D1187416

UNCAGED

Dave Krider,
J.R. Shelt,
and Scott Freeman

Foreword by Dean Smith

SP

SPORTS
PUBLISHING
L.L.C.

SportsPublishingLLC.com

ISBN-10: 1-59670-042-4
ISBN-13: 978-1-59670-042-0

Publishers: Peter L. Bannon and Joseph J. Bannon Sr.
Senior managing editor: Susan M. Moyer
Acquisitions editor: Noah Amstadter
Developmental editor: Doug Hoepker
Art director: K. Jeffrey Higgerson
Dust jacket design: Dustin J. Hubbart
Interior layout: Dustin J. Hubbart
Photo editor: Erin Linden-Levy

Sports Publishing L.L.C.
804 North Neil Street
Champaign, IL 61820
Phone: 1-877-424-2665
Fax: 217-363-2073
SportsPublishingLLC.com

Printed in the United States of America

CIP data available upon request.

To my sons, Randy and Brooke, who left this earth at much too young an age. Your mother and I love you both, and we miss you every day of our lives.

—DK

To my players—you have truly blessed my life. And to my family—thanks for the prayers and understanding. I love you all.

—JRS

To my parents, and my family, for their love and faith.

—SF

FOREWORD

BY DEAN SMITH

Jack Keefer is the only basketball coach in the history of
Lawrence North High School, so a book about the dynasty of the
program is actually one detailing the greatness of Jack as a coach as
well as the talents of the young men who have played for him.

When talking about Coach Keefer's career, be careful not to
pigeonhole him. He is the whole coaching package: strategist,
effective and patient teacher, fair, hard worker, competitor, and
loyal to his players and assistant coaches. Even in his 60s, he continues to maintain a fresh outlook on life and coaching, which is
conducive to learning and improving, and will continue to be, no
matter how long he decides to coach. He is a superb motivator
who knows all the tricks of the trade. He once had his team
brought to the school's theater department, where he dramatically
rose from a coffin to exclaim, "We're not dead yet!" (And they
weren't, as they went on to win the sectional!)

I've known Jack since 1979, when he began working our summer basketball camps at the University of North Carolina and continued working them through the 2000 season. Some coaches
come to these college camps to network and socialize, but Jack
came to work. He was so effective as a teacher and such a depend-
able leader that I immediately put him in charge of one of our
eight gyms, which was a coveted position at our camps.

Jack's coaching prowess and accomplishments will be detailed elsewhere in this book, but I will give brief highlights. His 2006 team ended the season ranked No. 1 in the nation, the first Indiana high school team ever to accomplish that honor. He was named 2006 National High School Coach of the Year by *USA Today*, *Sports Illustrated*, and the National High School Coaches Association. His school's winning streak reached 45 in a row at the end of the 2006 season, which ties an Indiana high school record that has been in place for over 50 years. Lawrence North finished the 2006 season undefeated at home for the fourth straight year. Jack has coached four state championship teams, including the last three in a row, which ties another state record.

Jack is a brilliant coach who has a reputation of being especially good at teaching big men. One of his former players, Eric Montross, was an All-American on our 1993 North Carolina team that won the national championship. While recruiting Eric, I watched Lawrence North play in the state regional against rival Pike. I witnessed a game that was managed brilliantly by both benches. Jack and Pike coach Ed Siegel could have handled any college game with the uncanny moves they made that day. It was an incredible game from start to finish. Lawrence North won by one point. Jack and Ed put on a coaching clinic, and rarely have I seen such intensity and desire at any level of basketball.

As a veteran coach, Jack has lost none of his intensity or his desire to be the best he can be. Players who can't stay out of the gym are referred to as "gym rats." Jack is still that way as a coach. He's in the gym year-round (generally by 6 a.m.), because he realizes that young players like to have daily contact with their head coach as well as the assistants. By the way, I think Jack would admit that one of the reasons for his great success is the loyalty shown by several of his long-time assistant coaches. Jack is smart enough to recognize his assistants' strengths, delegate responsibility to match these strengths, and give his assistants much freedom. I learned a lot from my assistant coaches during my 36 years as head coach at North Carolina, and Jack does likewise. It's to his credit that he's willing to listen to new ideas. Jack has excellent leadership skills and runs his program like any great CEO of a business.

Growing up in a one-parent home, Jack participated in sports as a youngster but also did odd jobs at every opportunity to help his mother and two sisters. He developed a strong work ethic early on that, in addition to a determination to rise above his circumstances, contributed significantly to his development as a great basketball coach. The product of a small Indiana high school, my guess is that few people predicted that Jack would become one of the best high school coaches in the history of this basketball-crazy state.

I realize that some competing coaches have accused Jack of recruiting talent, but I believe that is due to envy on the part of these coaches. It is also due to some players moving into his school district due to Jack's great reputation. If kids transfer—or move into his district at a young age—it's because they want to play for a coach who will get the most out of them. When a high school coach sends almost 70 of his players on to play college basketball, the word gets out about that coach's ability to teach and help his players excel. Young people want to play for a coach like Jack, who coaches at the highest level but also cares about his players as people.

Don't get the idea that Jack is all work and no play. He has a terrific sense of humor and often entertains his teams at his home.

Coaches find it handy to be able to laugh at themselves, a trait that Jack has perfected. This is particularly important as his propensity to forget names and at times display absentmindedness are legendary among those who know him best. However, his easygoing manner about some things should not fool you. When it comes to basketball and his players, Jack is entirely focused!

Jack's last four years coaching the Wildcats have been incredibly successful, led by stars Greg Oden, a 7-footer, and stellar point guard Mike Conley. But those who think Jack's program will decline greatly with the departure of Oden and Conley to college basketball haven't studied his coaching history. He had great players before Oden and Conley, and there will be others in the future, many of whom will reach heights they didn't dream of under Jack's superb coaching and teaching.

Jack's wife, Jan, hopes that he will continue coaching long enough to coach their grade-school son, Jake, at Lawrence North High. That would put Jack into his 70s and give him a shot at winning more games than any high school coach in Indiana history. I hope Jack continues coaching as long as he loves and enjoys it. The sport needs people like him, people who care about the game and also care about developing young men, as Jack does.

You might wonder if the basketball dynasty at Lawrence North will continue now that such extraordinary talent has departed. As long as Jack Keefer is the coach of the Wildcats, they will be one of the top programs in the state of Indiana and the nation. He's that good!

INTRODUCTION

BY DAVE KRIDER

In the fall of 2003, I was reading a preview about the upcoming Indiana high school basketball season, which included a portion about the Indianapolis Lawrence North team. The Wildcats had lost only three games the previous year—two to undefeated Class 4A state champion Pike—with two freshman starters leading the charge. According to the preview, 6-foot-10 center Greg Oden and point guard Mike Conley were seasoned sophomores and gave the team a great nucleus.

At the time, I was just getting my feet wet in book publishing. I turned to my faith in God for guidance, and He instilled in me a belief that this Lawrence North team could be special, a one-of-a-kind dynasty. That was my sole motivation for starting this book.

I called Lawrence North coach Jack Keefer and told him that I wanted to begin writing a book chronicling his current team. Since I lived in LaPorte, Indiana, about 150 miles north of Indianapolis, I asked if he had any interest in working on the book with me. I would do much of the background research and interviews; all I needed was someone to have their ear to the floor, and to keep a diary of the day-to-day life of the Lawrence North team. He suggested his assistant coach, J.R. Shelt, who was also an English teacher. The match made sense, so J.R. and I moved forward with the book.

The rest is so much more than history. The Wildcats won three consecutive Class 4A state championships, and were crowned national champions in 2006 by the likes of *Sports Illustrated*, *USA Today*, and the Associated Press. It has been a tremendous pleasure to watch this team play for three years. Not only were the Wildcats comprised of superior athletes and spectacular basketball players, they also featured top students and true gentlemen. A young kid growing up with his own hoop dreams could find no better role models than young men like Oden and Conley.

The 2005-06 Lawrence North Wildcats. Photo by David Dixon

ONE

Mike Conley set the tone from the first moment of the season.

What had come to pass was of little significance. All that mattered now was what lay ahead. It was of no concern that sportswriters had doled out thousands of words speculating whether the 2005-06 Lawrence North team would prove to be the best high school team in the history of Indiana basketball. Better than the Indianapolis Washington team from 1969 that George MacGinnis had led to a 31-0 record and a state championship. Better than the 1956 Crispus Attucks team that Oscar Robertson led to an undefeated season. Better than the 1920s Franklin teams that won three consecutive state championships. Even better than the Marion High teams that won three straight in 1985, '86, and '87, including one undefeated season.

Conley followed the lead of his coaches and insisted the state championships Lawrence North had won in 2004 and 2005 didn't matter now. He wanted nothing to do with the history they were chasing. "We're not after three," he told his teammates. "We're after *one*."

Greg Oden, the strapping, 7-foot center who was the top-rated high school player in the nation, fell right in with Conley. "Hey, we have championship rings," he kept reminding his upperclassman teammates. "But some of these kids coming up, they don't have one; we owe it to them to try and get *one*." Forget about the pressure of winning three straight. Forget about being touted as the No. 1 high school team in America in the pre-season. Forget about the blinding spotlight trained on Oden. *One* was the theme, the mantra, for the entire season. The team as one, together. Going after one championship. Let the rest fall into place from there.

Conley, a sleek, lightning-quick 6-foot-1 point guard, was the kind of player whom John Wooden would have loved to coach. Basketball smart. A team player. Not a selfish bone in his body. Conley always looked to pass and set up his teammates. He was a natural. There were periods where he seemed to lose interest on the court, like the act of leading a legendary basketball team came too easy for him. He was so good that he could sink 25 straight free throws in practice, and then he might miss the next five because he was bored with the exercise. He would temporarily lose focus, and the autopilot would kick on. But put pressure on Conley—tick him off—and he could take over a game.

The classic Mike Conley moment came during his junior year at one of Lawrence North's open-gym sessions, where basketball players show up on their own time to play pick-up games under the watchful eye of the coaches. Mike was going at it hard with his back-up, Tyler Morris. Morris was a tough-nosed kid who was able to secure a scholarship to Boston University even though he was a back-up for Lawrence North and didn't play many minutes. But in practice, he had enough game to push Conley, who was fielding interest from powerhouse programs like Wake Forest and Ohio State.

On this day, the dueling guards were trash-talking each other the whole game like a couple of competitive brothers. Late in the game, Conley's team was up one bucket. Morris came down the floor, pulled up, and drained a jump shot to tie the score. Conley dribbled down court and pulled up for a jumper about 26 feet from the basket. With Morris nearly inside Conley's jersey, Conley launched a high, arching shot. As soon as the ball left his fingertips, Conley turned and began to run off the court, turning his head back to yell out, "That's game." Nothing but net.

Coaching Conley was all about challenging him. And Jack Keefer, Lawrence North's head coach for the past 30 years, knew how to push Conley's buttons. He would tease Mike about Eric Gordon, a crosstown shooting guard for rival North Central High School with a smooth touch alá Glenn Rice. "Hey, Michael," Keefer would say when a game with North Central loomed. "They think you'll be the second best guard on the floor. Did you see where their coach said that in the paper? That Eric Gordon is the best guard in the country? Michael, don't you play guard? He's better than you, didn't you know that?"

A similar technique was employed with the big fellow, Oden. Well in advance of his senior year, he was already being projected as the No. 1 pick in the NBA draft. So it would have been very easy for Oden to coast through his senior season and await the fortunes ahead of him. But that was not in his nature. Oden had no posse, no Hummer, and no attitude. He was so down to earth and disinterested in image that he wore mostly sweat pants to school. He was a shy and unassuming kid who happened to be 7-feet tall, both athletic and mature beyond his years.

Oden and Conley were the first freshmen to ever start on a Jack Keefer team. To anyone who had ever watched them compete on the court, the reasons were obvious. Conley was well versed in the game of basketball; he'd had the fundamentals drilled into him until they were part of his DNA. On the court, he was a brilliant point guard and a born leader. Oden, meanwhile, was a man among boys. The heads of the players who guarded him seldom came past his shoulders. At times, he resembled a laconic hound dog surrounded by a batch of frisky pups, anxiously yelping at him but powerless to stop him from doing as he pleased. Oden could have scored 50 points a game. But like Conley, it was his instinct to involve his teammates, often passing up scoring opportunities to get others an open look at the basket. Oden sometimes took that mentality to the extreme, to the point that Coach Keefer had to scold him into shooting more often.

Scouts had already proclaimed Oden as a once-in-a-generation center. Another Mikan, another Chamberlain, another Alcindor, another Shaq. The only reason he wasn't already in the NBA was because he was still in high school. The only reason there wasn't a recruiting frenzy at Lawrence North was because college coaches had assumed Oden would turn pro after his senior year. And the only reason he wasn't in the middle of a LeBron James-style frenzy was because the NBA had just declared high school seniors ineligible for the draft. After the NBA instituted its new rule, Ohio State coach Thad Matta began a serious effort to land Oden and Conley. When Conley decided to commit to the Buckeyes, it seemed only natural for Oden to go there, too. After all, the two hardly knew what life on the court without the other was like. They had been teammates for six straight years. So why not another year or four in college?

But, for now, none of that mattered. They had an entire senior season ahead of them—the best year of their young lives. Their focus was clear: *One.*

Mike Conley (No. 42; middle row), Greg Oden (No. 50; back row), and their undefeated
2001-02 Craig Middle School teammates. Courtesy of Craig Middle School

TWO

Greg Oden was not a particularly large baby at eight pounds, nine ounces, and 19 inches long. However, he definitely had growth potential: His father, Greg Sr., stood 6-foot-3; his mother, Zoe, was 6-foot-1; and he had an uncle who was 6-foot-8. Greg didn't waste much time as a youth, progressing through growth spurts that surely caused his parents some pause when it came to purchasing clothes for their son.

Zoe recalls that her son was always taller than the other kids his age. "In fourth grade, he grew a lot," she says. "He got a little embarrassed about [his height]." Greg Sr., who operated a plumbing and heating business in Buffalo, New York, never projected his son to be a basketball star despite his height as a youth, but does recall that Greg ran like a deer thanks to his long legs. Up through age eight, Greg had developed no affinity for basketball. Height or no height, his family had never attempted to peak his interest.

The Odens divorced after 10 years of marriage when Greg was nine years old. Zoe packed up her belongings and drove Greg and his younger brother, Anthony, from Buffalo to Terre Haute, Indiana, where she had relatives. Attending fourth grade at Fuqua Elementary School in Terre Haute, Greg was a typical—though rather tall—kid. His parents both remember him as a quiet, pleasant child. He absolutely devoured Saturday morning cartoons on television, which soon sparked a love affair with movies. Like many youth, Greg was developing an addiction to TV. He would soon be blindsided by an unforeseen intervention.

During fourth grade, Greg was approached by a pair of coaches of a fourth-grade Amateur Athletic Union (AAU) basketball team, the Terre Haute Stars. John Gilmore and Jimmy Smith had been given a tip about a tall fourth-grader at Fuqua Elementary, so they sought out the school principal in the hope that she would speak with Greg on their behalf. That night, Greg took a business card home to his mother. He was interested in playing, but there was a catch: Saturday morning would have to be reserved for practice and games. He eventually chose wisely: basketball over television.

At his first practice with the Stars, Greg confessed to his new coaches that he had never played organized basketball. Coach Smith could tell after a few drills that Greg was telling the truth. He was a gangly 5-foot-8 and towered over other players, but on the court Greg was obviously lacking the skills of his experienced, hand-picked teammates.

"He really didn't understand the game," recalls Smith. "He did not know how to shoot and couldn't dribble. When he got a rebound, he would travel. He would stand in the lane and be whistled for three seconds."

Greg was, as they say, a work in progress. Footwork provided him with possibly his biggest challenge. Greg recalls—only half-jokingly—that the hardest thing for him was learning how to walk. "I was very awkward," he says. "I couldn't run and I had a lot of trouble with layups." At first, Greg even had a problem scoring in the correct basket. His first two points in organized basketball counted *for the opposing team.* Consequently, the lanky youngster didn't see much game action. He spent most of his time on the pine as a fourth and fifth grader.

What transpired during those first two years, however, showcased Greg's remarkable attitude, a trait he possessed even as a youngster. He never complained about his lack of playing time, and instead spent as much time in the gym as possible, working tirelessly to improve his game—layup after layup.

"I really didn't look at it like work," Greg recalls. "Jimmy Smith worked tremendously with me. I probably wouldn't be as dedicated today if it wasn't for him."

A little bribe here and there didn't hurt, either. Greg's mother always promised to buy him fish sticks or chocolate milk if he scored in the game. In the classroom, Greg didn't need any incentive to make good marks. He took great pride in his report card at each grading period, always making sure to show it to his coaches, who were impressed with Greg's intelligence and desire to be a success off the court. Likewise, it would have been easy for a kid who found success away from the court to become disinterested with a sport he couldn't master. But for Greg, the challenge was worth the wait.

Mike Conley might as well have been born with high tops on. Basketball was a part of his life from the tender age of 14 months, when he was given a Nerf basketball and a miniature goal as a Christmas gift. His parents—Mike Sr. and René—didn't have a clue at the time that they had just launched their son's life-long pursuit of basketball excellence. From that day on, the family rec room was the toddler's basketball court. As soon as his legs could support him—let alone keep up with him—he shot baskets every day, all day, neglecting his other toys and neighborhood friends in favor of that little Nerf ball.

Mike fed off his family's support, and his family's support grew out of his enthusiasm for basketball. His parents never forced basketball on their son, but the sport found him. And once it did, it would not let go of young Mike's imagination. His uncle, Steve Conley, who played linebacker for the Pittsburgh Steelers and was no slouch as an athlete, recalls his nephew, then just six years old, embarrassing him in a game of H-O-R-S-E in the driveway—with the rest of the family watching.

"He beat me with pure jump shots," recalls Steve Conley. "The competitor in me came out. I missed a layup and that really got me upset. Several adults were there and they laughed at me."

Another uncle recalls the ease with which young Mike would win prize after prize at the county fair, sinking shots at the basketball game while sitting on the counter. The poor carnie who roped little Mike into playing a game was transformed from town crier to speechless sucker.

Like so many kids growing up in the early-'90s, Mike wanted to be like Mike. And luckily for him, he had two Mikes to idolize: Michael Jordan and his own father. The elder Mike Conley was a former standout on the University of Arkansas track program who had earned a gold in triple jump in the 1992 Olympics. His success would shadow his son as he grew older, but as a youngster Mike found his dad's track career anything but impressive. Mike Sr. showed his son a videotape of him—as a collegian—finishing second in a 200-meter race against 1984 Olympic silver medalist Kirk Baptiste. Mike's reaction: tears. He was stunned that his father had lost, crying, "Daddy you lost!" over and over. Possibly little Mike picked up that desire to win from watching Michael Jordan. When he wasn't on the rec room court, he was often watching highlight tapes of his Airness.

Folks outside of the Conley family were also quick to notice something unique in young Mike. His mother, René, recalls the time a writer and photographer from *Sports Illustrated* visited the family at their home in Fayetteville, Arkansas, to interview Mike Sr. The four-year-old paid the visitors no mind; he was too busy shooting hoops by himself.

"Mike came out of the game room just sweating," his mother remembers. "[The folks from *Sports Illustrated*] were just so shocked at Mike's ability—how he could dribble and shoot a [regulation-size] ball."

Father and son started to develop a unique closeness when Mike was a second-grader. His father was asked to help coach the Arkansas Kings, an AAU team consisting of fourth graders. Mike Jr. was extended an invitation to play on the team—even though the other kids were two years older. The age gap was no matter; Mike was already more advanced than many of them. Playing for a private elementary school as a third-grader on nine-foot baskets, Mike exploded for an incredible 52 points in the Fayetteville city championship game.

"As a kid he didn't really care about scoring that much," Mike Sr. stresses, "but he wanted his team to win that championship so much."

Mike Sr. wasn't the only guide in young Mike's development. University of Arkansas head coach Nolan Richardson had a hand in shaping Mike as well at his summer basketball camp. Mike brought home lots of hardware in his four summers at Richardson's camp: MVP trophies and plaques for three-point accuracy and other offensive feats. The rec room was quickly turning into a trophy case.

Again, Mike was taking advantage of kids two years older than him. At camp, he reached the quarterfinals of a one-on-one contest, never allowing his lack of size or strength to deter him against older opponents. That boosted his confidence, and earned him a spot on Richardson's staff as a ballboy for Arkansas' home games.

"Little Michael was very active all the time—always on the move," Richardson remembers. "I watched him grow up, playing on outside courts. I could tell he was going to be a good player."

Mike knew what he wanted to do with a ball in his hands, and he made certain that it happened. He had all the intangibles—decision-making, instincts, IQ—readily apparent from a young age. He received his first nation-wide exposure at age nine as the leading scorer for his father's Arkansas Hawks, an AAU team that won the national 10-and-under crown. As a fifth grader, Mike won a citywide three-point shooting contest against a field that included kids several years older—and many adults. Because he won, he was allowed to shoot to win a car. All he had to do was sink a three-pointer—while blindfolded. Unfazed, Mike fired away. His shot bounced once on the rim, then twice, before falling to the ground. The older competition was saved further embarrassment.

Mike remained focused on the game as his father groomed him to be a gym rat. "I'd like to say I worked on specific things," says Mike, "but for some reason I already had mastered dribbling, passing—things like that. It just all seemed to come naturally. I was just blessed to be given that talent."

Basketball came so easily to Mike that he could score at will, as if the ability to shoot a jumper came as easily as flipping on a light switch. Possibly, that led to boredom on the court, because as he aged Mike became less interested in scoring, and more interested in seeing the play of his teammates improve. He would routinely pass up scoring opportunities in order to get others involved on offense. The results were spectacular, as father and son led the Hawks to the 11-and-under national crown—their second championship in a row. But dad didn't let his son grow too big for his britches. He preached humility, and Mike followed his lead just as he followed his dad to Indianapolis, Indiana, where the family relocated to start Mike's sixth-grade year. A whole new scene—with unknown players and first-time spectators waiting to have their minds blown—awaited Mike in the Hoosier state. For someone who breathed basketball and had a legendary competitive streak, this was like winning the lottery.

Entering sixth grade, Greg Oden had sprouted to 6-foot-2, added some weight, and began to advance rapidly through the "work in progress" stage. His understanding of the game was improving thanks to plenty of 5-on-5 practice sessions, and his natural athletic abilities were shaping him into a defensive force capable of altering the opponent's offensive game plan. All of a sudden, coach Jimmy Smith had a new weapon at his disposal. Greg was no longer a benchwarmer; he was quickly becoming the team's No. 1 option.

Basketball was providing young Greg with plenty of eye-opening opportunities, both on and off the court. Traveling with his AAU team to a tournament in Dallas, Texas, allowed Greg to check off a notable first—an airplane flight. As the plane took off, several girls screamed. Greg, meanwhile, grabbed his coach's arm as his eyes widened. "I'm sure he was scared to death," recalls Smith.

Greg's first look at an ocean came during another basketball trip to Cocoa Beach, Florida. "He was like a big stork out there in the water," Smith laughs.

At the same time Greg was slowly becoming a force to be reckoned with, Mike Conley Sr. was taking over the AAU Riverside Oddbreakers, an Indianapolis team his former AAU club had beaten in the national finals the previous summer. Fresh off a move from Arkansas to the Mecca of basketball that winter, Conley was desperate to add some height to his new team. He had all the ingredients of a great nucleus, except for a tall center. Greg was just the sort of rising sixth grader he was after. Other coaches warned him against pursuing Greg, however, telling him, "You don't want him. He limps up the floor and he barely plays for his own team."

But Conley really *was* desperate, so he worked out a deal with Coach Smith to add the developing center to his roster for area and national tournaments. During their first meeting, Conley asked Greg what he wanted to be when he grew up. Greg's response was hardly typical for an 11-year-old: a dentist. Conley looked at Greg's huge hands and exclaimed, "You're not going to put those hands in my mouth!"

While he had the body of a dominating center, Greg still had much to learn, especially now that he was playing with an even better AAU club. It was back to the bench when he played with his new team, which thrived thanks to their new point guard, Mike

Conley. Mike Jr. was a perfect fit on a team whose roster pulled primarily from the Pike High School district. The result was hardly surprising: a 12-and-under National AAU crown. As seventh-graders, Greg and Mike continued to play together on Conley Sr.'s new AAU team, Spiece Indy Heat, which won the 13-and-under National AAU title, marking the fourth straight year that the Conleys had taken the nation's top prize.

For two years, coaches Smith and Conley shared their budding big man. Smith is still grateful to the Conley family for picking up where he left off in making sure that Greg's development both on and off the court met high standards. Conley stressed many similar goals as Smith: work hard, build confidence, and improve offensively. The offensive side of Greg's game was lagging behind. He often subbed for Greg during games just so he could lay into him for passing up a good, open shot. Greg's confidence was still playing catch up to his actual skills. Coupled with his unselfish nature, his lack of faith in his shot caused further growing pains. He refused to take open 10-foot jump shots in games—even though he made those shots in practice. Greg chalks those former confidence issues in part up to poor vision. "I'm practically blind without my glasses or contacts," he says.

As a 6-foot-6 seventh grader, Greg was yanked from an AAU tournament game by Coach Conley for not putting forth his best effort. The next day, the team played its toughest opponent of the season, and Greg played the best game of his young career. He brought the crowd to its feet, in fact, by catching a pass at full speed and dunking with two hands. These were lessons learned for Greg.

The Oden family, which had become very close to the Conleys, moved 70 miles north to Indianapolis as Mike and

Greg entered eighth grade. Greg's mother yearned to live in a larger city and was able to secure a good job at St. Vincent Hospital. It seemed only natural for the Odens to choose to live in the Lawrence North High School district, because that's where the Conleys resided. The move was controversial for basketball reasons: Greg would have attended Terre Haute South High School, at the time coached by veteran Pat Rady, if not for the move. Terre Haute fans were ultimately disappointed in their loss. But Coach Smith—who was glad that Greg's family decided to move to Indianapolis—claims that the Terre Haute high school coaches failed to pay enough attention to Greg, so the move made sense.

It obviously was a matter of too little, too late, but Mike Saylor, who now is South's head coach, pleaded with Greg's mother for the family to remain in Terre Haute. "I don't think any of us knew much about him until he was a sixth grader," says Saylor. "We were really paying a lot of attention at that time. You could see he had very lively legs and feet and was going to be extraordinarily tall. I was telling everybody, 'This guy is going to be an NBA player.' I sure wish we'd paid more attention to him [earlier]."

The Oden-Conley Show was an instant hit at Indianapolis' Craig Middle School. Word spread quickly that something magical was happening on the basketball court, thanks in part to the new 6-foot-8 kid in school. Fans came out in droves to watch Mike lob passes to Greg for rim-rattling, fast-break dunks. After playing together for two summers, the duo shared a sort of telepathy on the court. "It's just Mike telling me what to do with his eyes," Greg explains. But just a year prior, Greg may have dropped those same alley-oop passes. This was a new and improved Greg Oden; he had finally arrived.

With their reactions in sync, Greg and Mike produced results that were at times astounding. Their eighth-grade team went undefeated, and often played before packed houses of 2,000 fans. "We were the talk of the town," Mike says proudly. "We were just dominating people."

The Oden-Conley chemistry really began to blossom at the end of their eighth-grade year, when they were invited to participate in various summer camps and tournaments. "We always stayed in the same room on the road and we bonded," Mike explains. "Our chemistry feeds on the off-court things."

Greg was on a fast track to becoming one of the Hoosier state's most heralded big men. Soon, the nation would learn why old-timers had taken to calling him a "young Bill Russell." Both Greg and Mike were invited to the prestigious Nike Jamboree Camp in St. Louis the summer before their freshman year. There was just one minor problem: Greg wasn't confident that he belonged there. Feeling that his offensive game wasn't ready for the national spotlight, Greg only reluctantly agreed to attend. Once there, however, his nerves settled as he quickly became the talk of the camp. Greg was close to nudging his name on the list of Indiana immortals that included Oscar Robertson and Larry Bird. Only time would tell.

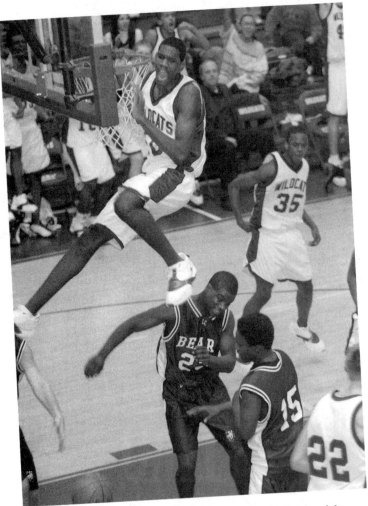

Freshman Greg Oden made an immediate impact. Mpozi Mshale Tolbert/*The Indianapolis Star*

THREE

Things were looking up for the Lawrence North basketball program in the fall of 2001. The previous year's varsity team had finished 21-6, and six players who would go on to play Division I college ball were returning from that squad. The team's shortest frontline player was 6-foot-7, and they also had a 6-foot-6 guard. Walking onto the court, the Wildcats looked more like a well-stocked small college team than a team playing high school ball in Indiana. Waiting in the wings was a bevy of much-hyped talent at Craig Middle School, a feeder school for Lawrence North. A tall eighth-grader by the name of Greg Oden was making quite the impression.

Despite high expectations, The Wildcats struggled out of the gate. Hoping to reverse his team's momentum heading into a matchup with Kokomo in the fourth game of the young season, Jack Keefer pulled aside assistant coach J.R. Shelt and asked him to deliver the pregame speech. Shelt was taken aback by the request. A graduate of Indiana State, where he was a walk-on player for the Sycamores before eventually becoming a starter, Shelt had worked as an assistant at a couple of schools in the area prior to transferring to a teaching job at Lawrence North, which was looking for African-American male teachers like himself who could serve as role models to its student body.

Shelt was a rookie on an experienced coaching staff, and Keefer was not known for passing the buck when it came to the pregame talk. Keefer left the locker room, leaving Shelt to fend for himself. He began to go over the game plan with the players, but was abruptly interrupted when Coach Keefer burst into the room clad in blue jeans, worn work boots, and a blue jean shirt. "Boys," he shouted, "I'm here to work." The message was genuine, even if the delivery may have missed the mark. But Lawrence North still lost 55-50, and the season quickly turned sour.

The most glaring problem for a team with so much talent was the lack of a point guard. Coach Keefer had to force-fit senior Stephen McDowell into the role. McDowell was a skilled, motivated player who would later sign to play for the University of South Carolina. Lawrence North usually had a distinct size advantage against their opponents thanks to 6-foot-9 center Andrejs Kregers, who would go on play at Ohio University. Yet McDowell, who was a scoring guard by habit, wouldn't get the ball to Kregers in the paint. McDowell had no experience as a point guard, and was resistant to adopting a pass-first mentality. He was simply out of place, playing a position where involving your teammates was essential. But the Wildcats had no reliable alternative. So they floundered, a team with no captain to guide its course.

The leader was supposed to be Angelo Smith, a 6-foot-7 forward who would receive a scholarship to play for Xavier University, whose head coach was Thad Matta. But Angelo's mother had passed away early in the school year, and the young man was overcome by grief. It was a tremendous burden for a teenager to carry, and the coaches knew it was a lot to ask of him considering the emotional rollercoaster he was on that season.

Without a leader to anchor them, the team's chemistry suffered. The Lawrence North players and coaches spend so much time together that if everyone doesn't get along, it's going to make for a miserable time. And the general consensus was that the 2001-02 season was miserable. Regardless of talent, the team never jelled and finished the season at a disappointing 11-11, the worst showing by a Jack Keefer-coached team in 15 years. The Wildcats' season ended with an embarrassing home loss in the sectionals to Indianapolis Arlington High School.

It would be the last home loss for the next four years.

Coach Keefer had heard talk all year long about the undefeated eighth grade team at Craig Middle School. But with his own team struggling to maintain a .500 season, Keefer and his coaching staff had enough on their minds. They were keeping tabs on their future players, but from a distance. Finally, late in the year, Craig had a showdown with another undefeated team: Lincoln Middle School, which fed Lawrence North archrival Pike. It was a matchup too good to ignore, so the Lawrence North coaching staff decided to attend the game.

Craig was missing one of its key players due to illness, and the Lawrence North coaches expected a close matchup. But Craig's players had other ideas. They quickly pulled ahead, never allowing

Lincoln an opportunity to get back into the game. Leading the charge was Craig's skinny 5-foot-10 point guard, Mike Conley, who took over the game by sinking shots, throwing crisp passes, and running the fast break. But his teammate, Greg Oden, was impossible to ignore. The Lawrence North coaches had heard plenty about Oden, who was being touted as the future of the Lawrence North basketball program, but this was their first opportunity to see him in action. At a little over 6-foot-8, Oden was long and lanky, barely weighing in at 200 pounds. He didn't have much to offer on offense, but treated the defensive paint as his private fiefdom. Anything that came in, he sent right back out.

The exclamation point in Craig's victory came when Conley began a fast break off his own steal. Oden sprinted down the court, trailing Conley. As Conley reached the basket, instead of going up for a shot, he tossed the ball off the backboard. Oden leapt, caught it, and slammed down a ferocious dunk. The Lawrence North coaches were in shock. Their single-word review was unanimous: "Wow!" They knew their world was about to change. It was obvious that Conley and Oden were major talents who were ready to play at the varsity high school level, right now. They played together with ease and determination, getting key stops when needed. And they were bolstered by the presence of a third wheel, Brandon McDonald.

The current prognosis was not pleasant for a mediocre Lawrence North team. But the future, well, that was bright.

Tryouts for the Lawrence North varsity boys basketball team are, in reality, over long before they start. Under Indiana High School Athletic Association rules, the formal tryouts are held over a three-day period in November. But the informal tryouts begin two or three weeks after the previous season is over. The competition in Indiana demands it.

The off-season at Lawrence North begins with open-gym sessions, pick-up games, and informal workouts supervised by the coaching staff. During the summer, there are morning workouts followed by weight training. Four days a week the kids have to be at the gym at 6 a.m., prepared to work for an hour and a half. That grind is the first proving ground.

The open gyms are always highly competitive, with as many as 45 kids hoping to make the 21-player roster. Usually, the 15 or so oldest players line up at one end of the court with Coach Keefer. At the other end are the remaining kids. The competition is denser for the freshman team, where 80 to 100 players fight for 15 roster spots.

Oden rarely, if ever, missed those 6 a.m. summer workouts. During scrimmages he showcased his surprising quickness and unselfish play, as well as his winning attitude; Greg never met a loose ball that wasn't worth diving for. Like Conley, Oden displayed a quiet humbleness that stood in stark contrast to all they had accomplished prior to arriving at Lawrence North. Oden, Conley, and McDonald quickly earned the respect of their older teammates. Junior guard Anthony "Penny" Sargent had taken on the team's leadership role, and he immediately embraced the newcomers. Sargent was the kind of leader the team needed, a hard-nosed kid who wasn't afraid to get in a teammate's face if necessary. Sargent's welcoming of the freshmen sent a message to the rest of his team: help has arrived, so be glad.

The big question for the Lawrence North coaches was not *if* these freshmen would make the roster, it was which upperclassmen would *not*. When it came time to make cuts and set the squad, the coaches noted that several seniors hadn't bothered to set a tone during open gym. One was a returning 6-foot-9, 300-pound center with a happy-go-lucky attitude and one speed—slow. With Oden now on the team, his primary role would be as Oden's practice opponent. Was he the kind of kid who would be able to push Oden? Another senior, forward Chaz Spicer, was a talented player but wasn't the hardest worker. The coaching staff debated cutting both and going without any seniors. They were concerned that the seniors would fail to set a good example for the freshmen. Without that leadership, their roles were greatly diminished.

The one certainty from the start was that Coach Keefer was going to do something he'd never done before—put a freshman in the starting line-up. In fact, he was going to start two: Conley and Oden. Due to his height and defensive presence, Oden was a no-brainer. Conley, likewise, was a must because of his steadiness and court intelligence. As evidenced by their mediocre play the previous season, the team needed a floor general, and Keefer felt Conley was up to the task.

Some of the parents of the senior players circulated a petition calling on Coach Keefer to sit Oden and Conley in favor of their kids. Needless to say, those kids were cut; Keefer didn't need that kind of distraction hanging over the season. The coaching staff also decided to cut the 6-foot-9 back-up center, and Spicer was on the chopping block until the very last minute. Coach Keefer had several conversations with Spicer's mother. The turning point came when she took her son to a department store and forced him to pick up a job application. "You're either going to work at basketball, or else work here," she told him. "One or the other. It's up to you." Spicer took the challenge to heart and earned a spot on the roster as the lone senior on the team.

In the coaching staff's mind, this would be a rebuilding year. They expected to improve upon the previous season, but not dramatically. The goal was to steadily improve and make a run when the state tournament sectionals began. Next year, they thought, they'd have a strong team with a seasoned senior presence.

But Conley and Oden—fresh off an undefeated season and accustomed to winning big—had other ideas. Losing wasn't in their vocabulary, and they had no intention of adding it at Lawrence North.

By his freshman year, Oden had grown to 6-foot-10 and was already generating significant attention. *The Indianapolis Star* profiled him in a feature story before he'd ever played a game in a Lawrence North uniform. Internet scouting Web sites were already touting him as the second best prospect in his graduating class of 2006. Scouts were calling him the second coming of Eric Montross, whom Coach Keefer had coached at Lawrence North in the late-'80s before he went on to star at North Carolina and then play in the NBA. Montross still held several Wildcat career records, including total points (1,874), most points in a single game (43), career rebounds (1,244), rebounds in a season (402), and rebounds in a game (22). "Montross was actually a little more awkward at that age," Keefer told reporters. "[Greg is] agile, and he just has a good feel for the game and likes to work. That's a combination that usually brings success."

Oden was still skinny, weighing just 210 pounds. But for a 14-year-old, his size—he wore size 19 shoes—was simply staggering. Opposing Indianapolis Pike coach Ed Siegel, now retired, colorfully described Oden the freshman as "a [big] baby robin flapping around—like he just got out of his shell." He hoped to put his size to good use for the Wildcats.

In the season opener, Lawrence North defeated Lawrence Central 62-48 in front of a standing-room-only crowd of 4,500 people. Oden scored the first points of his high school career with a dunk off of an alley-oop pass, and Sargent added nine early points as Lawrence North raced to a 20-8 lead. Sargent led the team with 17 points, and Spicer came off the bench for 16. Stefan Routt, the team's starting power forward, went down with an injury, which forced Spicer into his spot. In just a few weeks, Spicer had worked his way from almost being cut to the starting lineup.

Lawrence North won its first five games of the 2002 season before beating rival Indianapolis Arlington for victory No. 6, despite Arlington's decision to place pressure on the Wildcats' rookie point guard. Arlington opened the game with a full-court press and ran three defenders at Conley, thinking they'd scare him to death and force a turnover. Instead, Conley threw up a half-court lob to Oden for a dunk. On the bench, Coach Keefer looked over at his assistant, Jim Etherington, and said, "Wow!"

Arlington maintained pressure on Conley during the Wildcats' second possession. This time, Conley feigned a pass and used a burst of speed to shoot past the defenders. Coach Keefer again turned to Etherington to ask, "Did you teach him that?" Etherington shook his head. Keefer just shrugged. "I didn't either."

The Wildcats avenged the previous season's loss to Kokomo, now the seventh-ranked team in the state, to improve to 7-0. As Conley continued his rise as the floor leader that Coach Keefer had envisioned, Sargent became the team's offensive threat. Against Kokomo, the junior guard hit 12 of his last 18 shots to score 26 points.

In Indianapolis, the high school basketball season is marked by two events: the Marion County Tournament at mid-season, and the state tournament at the end. Lawrence North was still undefeated after it won its opening game of the county tourney on January 13, but then lost to a 9-2 North Central team in the quarterfinals, 69-63, despite a fierce comeback attempt in which the Wildcats hit 22 out of their last 38 shots.

It was the strangest game of the year, as North Central coach Doug Mitchell decided not to guard Conley, who had taken just three total shots in the two previous games. Instead, Coach Mitchell collapsed the defense around Oden in the middle. The move shocked Conley; no team had ever simply not guarded him. He was hesitant and unsure at the start, and North Central sprinted to a 16-2 lead. Finally, Coach Keefer instructed Conley to take advantage of the situation, and the freshman finished the game with six three-pointers and 21 points. Mitchell, who now calls Conley "the quiet assassin," learned a lesson.

But the rest of the Wildcat offense was ineffective. Sargent scored just four points, and Oden went scoreless. North Central also found success in the paint, attacking the basket all night long despite Oden's presence. Other teams had dared to drive on Oden, but they seldom did it twice after their first attempt was swatted away. But on this night, North Central had his number.

Coach Keefer seethed after the loss. He and Coach Mitchell had a personal rivalry that went back years. So losing to North Central was something that always gnawed at Keefer. The two teams were to hook up again in 10 days. In that time, Keefer taught his players how to run a 1-3-1 zone defense that was designed to stop North Central from driving. For the rematch, the Wildcats opened in their new defense, which closed off the lanes and took North Central out of its game plan. Conley sparked an offensive burst when he opened the game with two baskets, a pair of steals, and an assist. The Wildcats seized the lead, and never looked back, winning 69-53.

Nearing the end of the season, the Wildcats were ranked No. 2 in the state and faced a showdown with the No. 1 team, Pike High School. The matchup loomed large: Pike was undefeated and garnering comparisons to the greatest teams in Indiana high school basketball history. They featured an extraordinarily balanced attack; with as many as eight players expected to receive Division I basketball scholarships, their talent ran deep.

Playing in front of 3,000 fans on Pike's home court, Lawrence North readied itself for a war. The Red Devils took an early 13-4 lead, but the Wildcats battled back to take the lead at the end of the first quarter. With just over a minute left in the fourth, Pike went up by six and appeared to have the game in hand. Then Spicer scored off an offensive rebound, and the Wildcats quickly fouled a Pike player to stop the clock. The Pike player missed both of his free throw attempts, but Pike rebounded the second miss. After another Pike miss from the field, the Wildcats controlled the rebound with 40 seconds left. Lawrence North pushed the ball upcourt on the fast break, and Sargent drove to the basket, converting on a lay-up. Coach Keefer had the Wildcats pressure using a full-court press on the ensuing inbounds play, and sophomore guard Brandon McPherson forced a turnover that resulted in a lay-up by Spicer, who finished with a game-high 25 points. That tied the game at 58. Pike hit a go-ahead bucket with 5.7 seconds left, but McPherson was then fouled by Pike, and hit both of his free throws to send the game into overtime.

McPherson opened overtime with a three-point basket, but Lawrence North ran out of gas in the extra period. Pike went on a 10-2 run and won 75-67. Still, the Wildcats had gone into enemy territory to play a heralded team and battled them into overtime. Despite the loss, Coach Keefer was almost giddy after the game. "I've got a pretty good basketball team," he proudly told reporters. "We played like a junkyard dog tonight."

Lawrence North entered the state tournament sectionals with just two defeats, and faced Connersville in their first game. Oden didn't attempt a shot or score a point in the game, and he didn't have to. It was a blowout; the Wildcats jumped out to a 19-2 lead and held Connersville to astounding three-of-41 shooting (7.3 percent) for the game to win, 65-18.

But in the next game against Warren Central, the Wildcats received a rude awakening, falling behind 21-2 to start the game. They went on a run in the second quarter to close to within eight at halftime. Warren Central was still clinging to a 42-39 lead at the end of the third quarter, when the Wildcats' lone senior, Spicer, put the team on his back and scored 10 of his game-high 22 points. The Wildcats went on a 12-0 run in the fourth quarter to put the game away with a 55-51 victory that earned Coach Keefer the 500th win of his career. "We used everything we've got to come back in that game," he said afterwards. "But I really liked that even though we fell way behind, we kept our composure."

The next evening, the Wildcats won their sectional by dismissing Indianapolis Cathedral, 60-37. With a couple of minutes left in the game, Lawrence North's student cheering section began to chant, "We want Pike! We want Pike!" The much-anticipated rematch would take place next, in the first round of the state regionals.

The pregame storyline was easy: The upstart Wildcats were the only school capable of stopping a Pike team that was defeating opponents in the state tournament with ease, assuring them of legendary status in Indiana hoops folklore. The matchup between the state's No. 1 and No. 2 high school programs at Hinkle Fieldhouse was considered the de facto state championship game, and 8,315 people showed up to watch the showdown at high noon on a mid-March Saturday.

There might not be a more storied basketball facility in the United States than Hinkle Fieldhouse, previously known as Butler Fieldhouse. The venue was once described by Bob Costas as "the Wrigley Field of basketball." When the 15,000-seat building was built on the campus of Butler University in 1928, it was the largest sports arena in America. Built with brick and mortar and featuring exposed metal beams inside, Butler Fieldhouse was once the epicenter of Indiana high school basketball. With the exception of a few years during World War II, every state championship game had been played there from 1928 until 1971. Walk into the fieldhouse for the first time, and you expect to see Gene Hackman handing a measuring tape to a couple of his players to check the length of the free throw line, then the height of the basket, before telling them with satisfaction, "I think you'll find them to be the exact same measurements as our gym back in Hickory." Butler was, after all, the ispiration for the setting of the fictional championship game in the movie *Hoosiers.*

It was at Butler that Oscar Robertson and his Crispus Attucks team became the first all-black high school in the country to win a prep championship in 1955. Butler was also the scene for the most famous high school basketball game in history. Bobby Plump hit a winning shot with seconds left in the game to give the Milan Indians—a high school of 161 students—the 1954 state championship over state powerhouse Muncie Central. It was the game that inspired *Hoosiers.*

Such a setting was not lost on the Lawrence North team as they arrived at Hinkle, ready to avenge their previous loss to the Red Devils. From the opening tip, Pike's offense was firing on all cylinders. They built a comfortable 51-36 lead with less than five minutes to go in the game. But Lawrence North wasn't going out without a fight. The Wildcats came storming back thanks to an 8-0 run to pull to within seven points with 1:58 remaining. Pike maintained its composure down the stretch, however, and held on for a 55-47 victory.

The loss was both frustrating and encouraging for the Wildcats. The frustration stemmed from Oden's inability to convert key shot attempts. He continued to miss lay-ups and "gimme baskets," in part because he was being fouled on each attempt. His woes continued at the free-throw line, where he failed to convert his free shots. The Wildcats lost by eight points; Oden was 0-9 from the line. A few made free throws could have tilted the game's momentum to Lawrence North. But even though the Wildcats lost, the team finished 21-3 on the season with an inexperienced group of players. They had achieved far more than anyone imagined in what was supposed to have been a rebuilding season.

Lawrence North fans were anxious for next season. The coaches were, too. Oden and Conley would be a year older with a year of high-intensity Indiana high school ball under their belt. More importantly: they had tasted defeat for the first time in a while, and found it to be sour. They were ready to rid that taste from their mouths. Off-season workouts would begin in just two weeks. The real season of promise was about to begin.

Brandon McPherson, left, and Stefan Routt. AP/WWP

FOUR

Defensively, Greg Oden was already an elite player as a freshman. His greatest gift—other than his 6-foot-10 wingspan—was his ability to stay planted on the court until his opponent made his move. The knack to know when to jump is the hallmark of all dominant shot blockers. They never leave their feet early; they lie in wait like a cat until the precise moment to spring. Offensively, however, Oden's game was still lacking. His first instinct when the ball was passed to him on the low block was to pass it right back out. His teammates loved that, but it didn't exactly work to the team's benefit to have a nearly 7-foot center who refused to shoot.

Oden was a tremendous athlete with all the tools coveted in a big man: mobility, good hands, plus-size. He could almost touch the top of the backboard from a standing jump. And he was a smart player. In so many ways, he was the total package. But on the offensive end of the court, he still lacked the necessary confidence and knowledge to become a scoring threat. He'd averaged a solid nine points and nine rebounds a game as a very green freshman. Most around him felt that with experience and coaching, he would blossom as a sophomore.

Coach Ralph Scott, the longest-tenured assistant on Coach Keefer's staff, put together a very detailed plan to awaken Oden's talents with the ball. Together, the two spent countless hours shooting face-up jumpers, half-hooks, banks off the glass, and jump shots from the baseline. Scott taught Oden to be aware of which players were collapsing on him in a double- or triple-team, and how to pass out of the defensive trap to find an open teammate for an uncontested basket.

One thing Scott didn't have to coach was desire, because Oden had plenty of that. What little effort he may have lacked on occasion was boosted by Coach Keefer, who demanded that Oden become a well-rounded player. There was one discussion between the coaching staff about whether Oden should switch off on picks in the open court. To do so would mean he'd be left guarding a smaller and quicker guard. Would it be smarter to allow him to stay put on his man and let the Wildcat guard try to fight his way through the pick? Keefer was adamant about the answer: Oden should make the switch. "I'm not going to make Greg a stiff," he exclaimed. "He's going to have to go guard people out there one day, and he might as well start now."

As raw as Oden was on the offensive end, there was no denying that he had spectacular potential—the sort that garners comparisons to legends and fills scouts' notebooks with an endless stream of superlatives. Privately, his coaches called him the most talented center in Marion County—Indiana Pacers included. Some colleges began to scout him, although many didn't bother to waste their time, as Oden was already being touted as a lock to skip college and enter the NBA draft straight out of high school.

During the summer between his freshman and sophomore seasons, Oden, along with Mike Conley, competed in the annual Nike Basketball Camp, which draws the top 200 high school players in the country. The camp is held in July, the month which signals the official NCAA evaluation period, where college head coaches can evaluate prep players but still can't speak to them. At such all-star events, players participate in offensive-minded games on the court, while being lectured off the court on skills they'll need as they become basketball celebrities. In a classroom setting, high schoolers learn proper etiquette and are taught interview skills to prepare them for the media spotlight that engulfs the fast-paced, speculation-driven world of college recruiting.

Later that year during their basketball season, Duke University came to Indianapolis to play in the annual John Wooden Classic. Duke coach Mike Krzyzewski and Coach Keefer were already very familiar with each other because one of Keefer's former players, Andy Means, was on the Duke squad. Keefer took his team to Conseco Fieldhouse to watch Duke practice before their game. There, Coach K shocked Keefer by informing him that he wasn't going to recruit Oden. "You know, kids like that, if they're any good, they go pro," Krzyzewski told him.

Oden had but to prove he was "any good."

Going into the 2003-04 season, the respected *Hoosier Basketball* magazine named Lawrence North its preseason No. 1 team in the state. In doing so, the magazine had painted a giant red bull's-eye on the Wildcats' back. But Coach Keefer didn't mind—he relished the challenge and savored being the top dog. The status motivated the competitor in him, forcing him to work even harder to keep his opponents from knocking his team off that pedestal.

"I'm looking forward to this year," Keefer told *The Indianapolis Star*. "On paper, we look very good." Indeed they did. The only significant loss from the previous year's squad was senior Chaz Spicer, and Coach Keefer had sophomore Brandon McDonald—Oden and Conley's teammate at Craig Middle School—ready to step in. "When you have a team that's mostly back and been down this road," Keefer concluded, "you can drive them a little harder."

And drive them he did. During one of the early practices, Coach Keefer blew up at the team for not taking care of the ball; he was so angry that he couldn't even speak coherently. Of course, when Keefer became enraged, it was most often a calculated decision. He seemed to instinctively know when his team needed a kick in the rear, and he always did so in a way that drew their attention without getting nasty or personal.

After that practice, Keefer huddled with Stefan Routt, a senior power forward he was counting on to be a stabilizing influence on the court. Routt was feeling the pressure from junior forward Donald Cloutier, who was hot for his spot in the lineup. The two were best friends, but on the court they were still competitors. Cloutier had begun to receive Division I scholarship offers based on his play during open-gym sessions that summer. Routt, meanwhile, had not played well all summer. As a junior, Routt had averaged 8.6 points and 5.2 rebounds a game before a mid-season injury saw him lose his spot to Spicer. Since then, Routt's game had fallen apart. His jump shot wasn't falling, and it was affecting his confidence—as well as the rest of his game.

Coach Keefer knew Routt was already feeling down, so rather than confronting the kid, Keefer asked Routt a direct question: "What are you going to give us this year?"

"Rebounds, aggressiveness," Routt replied.

"Just offer us consistency," Keefer told him. "You may have to do all of the dirty work this year. Be that steady force with us on your shoulders."

The shot of confidence from his coach worked wonders. The next day, Routt had his best practice in weeks. It was as if the burden to recapture his form had been lifted from his shoulders because Keefer had told him, essentially, to give the team his best effort and let the rest take care of itself.

Effort was the word of the day for the team's preseason scrimmage against Pendleton Heights High School, a Class 3-A team located about 20 miles northeast of Indianapolis. Pendleton Heights played a motion offense that would make the Wildcats work hard on defense. They also had a 6-foot-9 center expected to test Oden, who had blossomed over the summer into a 6-foot-11 frame carrying 245 pounds. But the opposing big man proved to be of little concern for Oden, who dominated the scrimmage with 20 points on 10-of-14 shooting, and 10 rebounds. On one play, Oden took the ball at the foul line, faked to his left, and dribbled to his right. He took two long steps, powering through the lane, and went up for a ferocious dunk that brought the crowd to its feet. On another play, he ducked down into the paint and Conley fed him a touch pass. Oden caught it and delivered a one-handed flush. Later, he caught the ball on the block and executed a Chris Webber-like spin move for a two-handed dunk. Oden's long hours with Coach Scott were paying off; suddenly, with the ball in his hands, he was instinctively moving with purpose. What a difference a summer could make.

Despite the progress of their star player, Lawrence North coaches walked away from the scrimmage complaining that there were still so many things they had to work on: The Wildcats had played loose on defense; Pendleton Heights was more competitive than they should have been; Lawrence North should dominate any 3-A team. It hardly registered to any of them that Lawrence North *had* dominated, winning the scrimmage 79-40.

A week before the first game of the season, the school held a pep rally to kick off the season. Coach Keefer shaped the rally into his version of the NBA All-Star Weekend. The four-and-a-half-hour event featured a three-point shooting contest and a slam-dunk contest. (Brandon McPherson won the former, Penny Sargent the latter.) The cheerleaders even shot some free throws, and then students who had purchased $1 raffle tickets were invited to try their hand at the charity stripe.

It was a far cry from just two years earlier when Coach Keefer had stopped a Lawrence North pep rally cold to call out the seniors in front of everyone. A screaming "senior section" in the stands at courtside is a tradition in Indiana basketball. Lawrence North was accustomed to having a couple hundred kids in their senior section with a certain amount of spirit at every game. But during the team's 11-11 season two years before, the seniors had lost their enthusiasm. At a late-season pep rally, Keefer took the microphone and with authority, shouted, "You seniors, you suck." As gruff as that declaration was, the truth was, they *did* suck. They weren't supporting their school, and he didn't intend to let them get away with it.

The success of the 2002-03 season had brought back the passionate crowds. First, there was the early anticipation about Oden and Conley's freshman season. As the year went on and the wins racked up, the anticipation turned into enthusiasm. And it had only escalated entering this season. Thoughts of winning the state title—which hadn't happened since 1989, a long 14 years ago—had Wildcat fans riled up.

Outsiders were taking notice, too. The very afternoon of the pep rally, Oden was approached by MTV to do a *True Life* episode. He declined. He had no interest in climbing aboard the celebrity machine and becoming the next LeBron James. Besides, Oden didn't even consider himself the best player on the Lawrence North basketball team. That sort of humbleness was genuine. His teammates were continually awed by it. After being named MVP at the prestigious Challenge of Champions game his junior year, Oden gave his trophy to teammate Brandon McPherson, who had scored 19 points in the tournament's championship game despite playing with a leg injury. It was Oden's attitude, more so than his supreme talent, which inspired his teammates, many of whom have boasted they would run through the proverbial brick wall for him.

The night after the pep rally, the team went down to Bloomington to meet then Indiana University head coach Mike Davis, and to watch the Hoosiers play. After the game, Davis gathered the Wildcat players together and spoke to them. He obviously wanted to recruit Oden and Conley for his program, but it was Warren Wallace, a 6-foot-3 defensive specialist, who had worked to impress Davis.

"Next time you come down," Davis teased Wallace, "tell the ladies I'm your uncle."

"Yeah, we do look alike," Warren shot back before walking away with Davis' phone number.

It was not the first time in which Oden and Conley had attracted attention for the rest of their teammates. Nor would it be the last.

As the season opener neared, Coach Keefer became noticeably nervous and uptight. The last time he had coached a top-ranked team was in 1999, a winning but ultimately heartbreaking season for the Wildcats. Lawrence North should have taken the state title that year, and most likely would have if tragedy had not struck.

John Stewart was a 7-foot, 280-pound center in his senior year. With a basketball scholarship in hand from the University of Kentucky, Stewart was a talented player who had helped the Wildcats dominate their opponents throughout the season. Heading into the regional finals ranked No. 2 in the state, Lawrence North was ready for its biggest challenge yet—top-ranked Bloomington South. In front of almost 7,000 fans, the two teams battled to a 31-31 tie in the third quarter when Stewart pulled down an offensive rebound and put back the miss to score his tenth point of the quarter, and 22nd of the game. Seconds later, Stewart signaled to Keefer that he wanted to come out of the game. Keefer called a time-out. Stewart sat down on the bench, and collapsed.

Paramedics frantically worked on Stewart, while his team formed a circle on the court. After an ambulance took Stewart to the hospital, the team told Coach Keefer they wanted to finish the game. Following a 32-minute delay, the players went back out on the court. Bloomington South won 55-50 in overtime, but it hardly seemed to matter. After the game, Keefer told reporters he'd heard reports that Stewart was in stable condition. Moments later, a reporter for *The Indianapolis Star* was informed that Columbus Regional Hospital had just confirmed that Stewart had died. He pulled Keefer aside as the coach prepared to board the team bus, and broke the news to him. The coach began sobbing and walked into the bus. "John was the neatest young man I've ever coached," a stunned Keefer told reporters later at the hospital. "This is probably the low point of my life."

Doctors determined that Stewart had a rare cardiac condition called hypertrophic cardiomyopathy (HCM), which causes an enlarged heart. The normal treatment is to recommend the patient refrain from strenuous physical activity. HCM is an inherited disorder and can cause abnormal heart rhythms, which can result in a fast heartbeat and sudden death.

Kids that young aren't supposed to die, especially on a basketball court, especially someone like Stewart—a talented, passionate, warm person. The death affected the entire team. Coach Scott was probably the closest team member to Stewart because he coached the team's big men. But the death seemed to hit Keefer the hardest, because he considered all his players as his children. Stewart's death seemed to physically age Coach Keefer almost instantly. Looking at photos of him before 1999 compared to photos taken afterward, the difference is profound.

Now four years later, the emotions of being ranked No. 1 overwhelmed Keefer with joy and anxiety. This was a new team, but it brought about old feelings in him—thoughts of John Stewart and what could have been for that 1999 team. In an eerie similarity, Penny Sargent, the senior leader of the 2003 team, had suffered a heart murmur and had to undergo a battery of tests and a complete physical every summer before being cleared to play. Keefer kept a close eye on him. He wasn't about to let tragedy strike twice.

Keefer put the team through a short practice the day before their season opener, then met with them for 45 minutes to remind them of expectations. "No matter who you're playing and no matter how you feel, you go out and give your best," he told his players. "You don't make excuses for how you play. That's the kind of attitude I want from my team."

As is tradition, the Wildcats opened the season against Lawrence Central, and 3,500 fans crowded into the Lawrence Central gym to see the preseason No. 1 team. The Wildcats sent out Conley, Oden, McPherson, Sargent, and Routt—two sophmores, a junior, and two seniors—to start the game. Lawrence Central double- and triple-teamed Oden from the start, but the Wildcats struggled with their outside shooting and failed to take advantage from the perimeter. Conley was 0-5 from the field in the first quarter, and when it ended, Coach Keefer implored his team to settle its nerves and just play. "Step it up, guys!" he told them. The team settled down in the second quarter and cruised to an impressive 67-38 victory. Conley finished with 16 points, four steals, three assists, and a spectacular play worthy of the highlight reel. With 11 seconds remaining in the first half, he stole the ball at the baseline corner, passed the ball up court, sprinted down the court, shook the defense, set up in the corner, and nailed a nothing-but-net three-point shot at the buzzer. That play put Lawrence North up 34-17 at the half, and tore out the heart of the Lawrence Central team.

After the game, Oden was almost despondent. His father and grandfather had come down from upstate New York to see him play, and he hadn't received many touches. He didn't score until the third quarter, and finished the game with just three points. Oden wasn't embarrassed by his poor game simply because his family was in the stands; rather, he felt that he hadn't done enough to ensure that his team won. He was upset that his lackluster performance could have cost his team the win. As Coach Keefer had hammered into his players' heads, winning was about putting forth your best effort, and Oden was let down by his own offensive play.

The always stoic and self-contained center surprised his teammates with his postgame reaction. It was the first time any of his teammates had seen him visibly upset. He looked so depressed, sitting with his head down. Conley walked over to him and put his arm around Oden's broad shoulders. "Greg," Conley said, "you don't have to score for us to win." With that simple comment, a figurative light bulb flicked on in Oden's mind: Really? I don't have to score for us to win? Well ... okay, *we did* win by 29 points.

Next up was Brebeuf Jesuit High School, a 3-A team. At halftime the Wildcats were up by just three points, and Coach Keefer was not a happy man. "What are the two things we want to accomplish on offense?" he asked his players in the locker room. "One is to run the quickies [fast breaks]. What is the second?" He waited for someone to answer and when no one did, Keefer lost it. "Where have I gone wrong?" he screamed. "For two years, no, for 28 years I have not changed. If you guards won't run the lane to get the lay-ups and easy baskets, then you'd better pass the ball inside. And if you don't like it, go play somewhere else." With that, he walked out and left the team to contemplate the second half.

They responded in a big way, scoring the first nine points of the third quarter en route to a 13-point victory. And they did it with the sort of balanced attack that surely caught their coach's eye. Oden led the way with 14 points and 10 rebounds; Conley added 10 points and five assists; and Sargent and McPherson both chipped in 11 points.

After dispensing of Terre Haute South with ease, Lawrence North looked forward to a matchup with Marion High School, a team expected to fare well against the Wildcats due to their hulking, 6-foot-9, 285-pound center, T.J. Jones. But the game was a bit of a letdown, as Keefer's squad won by 15 points. Marion elected to play a zone defense, essentially telling the Wildcats they didn't trust their big man to guard Oden alone. Against the zone, Oden scored 14 points; his real test would come after the game. As his teammates milled around the court waiting to board the bus, Oden sat alone in the locker room, reluctant to leave. Somebody had told him that autograph seekers were waiting for him outside.

Assistant coach J.R. Shelt went in to speak with Oden, who told the coach of his situation, and how signing autographs seemed too … *weird*. Shelt corrected him. "You mean more to these kids than you realize," he told Oden. "Just go out there and sign those autographs, and then get on the bus." Oden did as he was told, signing his name over and over again until his hand began to hurt. Thus began a ritual that would happen at the end of every game from that point forward.

Whether he liked it or not, Oden was becoming a star. The reasons ran deeper than his willingness to embrace the fans off the court; on the court, he was blossoming. Against Warren Central, he started the game with a spin move that became a three-point play when he was fouled, then minutes later added a dunk off an alley-oop pass from Sargent. He finished that game with 19 points and 11 rebounds. Against undefeated Arlington in the sixth game of the season, he blocked four shots in the first eight minutes—setting the tone for the game—as Lawrence North broke out to a 16-4 lead. Arlington failed to score a field goal in the first quarter, and lost the game by 19 points.

Even though plenty of college coaches had been attending Oden's games, NCAA rules stated that recruiters couldn't make verbal contact with him until the end of his sophomore season. Like Duke coach Mike Krzyzewski, many coaches believed Oden would go straight to the NBA from high school. Plenty of recent evidence suggested that a gifted 7-foot high school center with plenty of upside would be a lock to be a lottery pick in the NBA draft. Two days before the Arlington game, a coach from the University of Michigan came to a Lawrence North practice to watch Oden, Conley, and Donald Cloutier. The coach told Keefer that he would love to have Oden, even if it was only for one year. And he encouraged Keefer to advise Oden to go to college for at least one year. "I would hate to think that I would have given up my freshman year in college just to travel around the country and play basketball," he said. Of course, if Oden attended college instead of entering the draft, he would be postponing—and risking the loss of—a hefty paycheck. Lottery draft picks were guaranteed a multimillion-dollar contract.

Oden's mother was already bracing for the gathering storm. "It's going to be tough to shield him," Zoe Oden told *The Indianapolis Star*. "I really don't think I'll be able to stop it. It hasn't been too bad so far. But we've had reporters call the house, which is rude. People keep telling me to let go, let him grow up." She shook her head and smiled. "He's still my baby."

Lawrence North's first real test of the year came in a showdown with the No. 2-ranked Columbia City Eagles at the City Securities Hall of Fame Classic two days after Christmas. But first, the Wildcats had to win a preliminary game earlier in the day against Northview High, which featured Logan Whitman, a 30-points-a-game scorer who later committed to play ball at Indiana State. Lawrence North concentrated its pregame practices on shutting down Whitman and defeating Northview—which they did, 76-64, with Oden scoring 23 points—and hadn't prepared sufficiently for their game against Columbia City later that evening.

The Wildcats faced a very deliberate, sharp-shooting team in the Eagles. Columbia City's offensive attack consisted of good ball movement and smart shot selection. Lawrence North tried to disrupt Columbia City by pressing, but the Wildcats didn't have the required energy to sustain an effective press due to their earlier game. With two minutes to go, Lawrence North was down by seven points with their undefeated season and No. 1 ranking on the line. Brandon McDonald became the hero as the clock wound down by tipping in a basket on an out-of-bounds play, then stealing the ball on defense. His steal led to a three-pointer that cut the Eagles' lead to two points. Conley sank two free throws to tie the game at 43-43 with 1:22 left in the game. Sargent had a chance to win the game in regulation, but missed a wide-open three-point attempt.

Lawrence North took the lead in the overtime period, and held a slim margin at 50-48 with seconds to go. Oden leapt high enough to alter a Columbia City three-point shot, but the Eagles tipped in the rebound at the buzzer to force a second overtime. Columbia City had built a slight 55-54 lead with 20 seconds remaining. Stefan Routt missed a shot with eight seconds on the clock, but Oden grabbed the rebound and was fouled. He calmly hit both free throws. Then Columbia City missed a last-second shot, and the battle belonged to Lawrence North.

"Our kids grew up a lot," Coach Keefer told reporters after the game. ". . . In the second game of the day to come back and play that hard . . . that's a mental toughness thing. I wasn't sure we could play that mentally tough."

The victory also taught Keefer that Lawrence North was vulnerable to opponents willing to slow the tempo in their favor. Keefer was the kind of coach who wanted his teams to get up and down the court in a hurry—his team's best shot against the opponent's best shot. The stall was becoming a tactic more and more opponents were using to try to slow down the Lawrence North express.

Less than a week later, the Wildcats faced their stiffest competition yet. One of the best teams in the Midwest, Detroit Renaissance High School, ranked No. 8 in the nation by *USA Today*, would square off against Lawrence North at the Challenge of the Champions Tournament held at Hinkle Fieldhouse. Lawrence North was going in without suspended guard Joe Ash, a defensive specialist. Coach Keefer worried about how his team would do against a powerhouse opponent with an astounding offense. The two teams had exchanged game film, and Detroit Renaissance had selected a game in which they murdered their opponent by a ridiculous score, something like 115-30. The Detroit squad featured two McDonald's All-Americans: 6-foot-4 guard Joe Crawford, who would later play for the University of

Kentucky; and 6-foot-6 guard Malik Hairston, who signed with the University of Oregon. With two supreme offensive talents, Coach Keefer never expected Detroit Renaissance to stall on offense—but that's exactly what they did.

Even though Detroit Renaissance was up 50-49 at the beginning of the fourth quarter, they couldn't contain Oden down the stretch, and they were bothered by the 1-3-1 zone trap defense that Lawrence North had sprang on them. And so they decided to hold the ball for as long as possible, hoping to neutralize the Wildcats' offensive attack and minimize turnovers on their own end of the floor. Lawrence North was still within a point late in the game. In the final two minutes, however, Oden twice went to the free-throw line, and twice missed both shots. Detroit Renaissance pulled out a 58-55 win, but Keefer took heart from the loss and the fact that the Wildcat defense had forced an explosive team to employ a stall tactic.

Lawrence North had just intimidated the eighth-best team in the nation.

Anthony "Penny" Sargent (No. 30) releases a shot. Indiana High School Athletic Association, Inc.

FIVE

The Monday following the loss to Detroit Renaissance, Coach Keefer put the team through a hard practice that concentrated on defense. The Wildcats hadn't played effective help defense against Detroit Renaissance, who spread out on offense and penetrated for too many easy lay-ups. Keefer wanted to get that squared away. And he had something else to get squared away— Greg Oden at the free throw line.

It is a well-known phenomenon in basketball that tall men are often awkward free throw shooters. Most are not good jump shooters period, in part because it is difficult for them to get the proper arc on the ball. But Coach Keefer wanted to make sure that Oden didn't become a fourth-quarter liability at the line, owning the same handicap that had marred the careers of extraordinary big men like Shaquille O'Neal and Wilt Chamberlain. If Oden couldn't nail free throws in the last minutes of a game, opposing teams were going to make his team pay. Had Oden hit even 50 percent of his free throws in the final two minutes against Detroit Renaissance, the Wildcats would have won.

Coach Keefer ended the practice by putting Oden into a pressure free throw situation: Lawrence North was down by one, a few seconds were left on the clock, and Oden was at the line. If he hit the free throws, the Wildcats won; if he missed, they lost. Oden walked to the line and set himself. He dribbled, lifted the ball, released the shot, and missed. Keefer forced the entire team to run. Then Keefer put Oden back in the same situation. He missed again, and again the entire team was forced to run. Oden went to the line for a third time. He missed. The team ran again. Finally Oden hit one. Then another. And another. At last, Keefer told everyone to go home.

The learning process continued in the next game against Franklin Central. The Wildcats built a quick lead, but Franklin Central started to make a run. Oden came to the Lawrence North bench and told Coach Keefer, "We need a time-out to regroup." Keefer told him to keep playing, and they eventually put an end to the run. At halftime, Keefer explained why he didn't call for the time-out. "I wanted someone to take charge and get us regrouped," he told his players. "I could have called a time-out and done it myself, but I wanted it to come from one of you."

Keefer never liked to call the first time-out of a game, and he hated to call time-outs when his opponent was making a run because he didn't want to let the other team know he was sweating. But even more, he wanted his leaders—Oden and Conley—to take charge on the court. He pulled the pair aside later. "If you think we need a time-out, have the balls to call time-out yourself," he said.

"Why do you need me calling it? If I call time-out, what does that do? It just stops the clock. You can't gather your thoughts out there? You can't get the team together? I want to see some leadership skills."

Keefer wasn't going to baby his star players. He knew they would be leading the team once senior Penny Sargent graduated, and they had to learn how to do it. "So what if a team makes a run? Do something to overcome it," Keefer told them. "Don't wait around for your coach to bail you out; he can't go out there and make shots. You let them make the run, so you stop it."

It was an important point to make because the 85th annual Marion County Tournament was right around the corner, and Lawrence North would face its stiffest stretch of games in the season. To get through their bracket to the championship game, the 10-1 Wildcats would have to go through either Pike, the No. 2-ranked team in the state, or North Central, the No. 3-ranked team. Both teams were 9-1; Pike had lost only to North Central. If the Wildcats survived that gauntlet, Warren Central, 7-1, loomed in the bottom bracket. Its lone loss that season was also thanks to Lawrence North.

Things got off to an ominous start when Oden twisted his ankle in practice only a couple of days before the tournament started. He missed the first game against Beech Grove, as did Joe Ash, who sat out the third game of his suspension. Without Oden, Lawrence North seemed lost. They struggled throughout the first quarter, down 14-12 at its conclusion. But to Keefer's delight they regrouped in the second quarter, jumping ahead 36-24 at the half with Donald Cloutier and Warren Wallace filling in for Oden. In the end, the Wildcats won going away, 73-46. But they received a taste of what life without Oden was like, and the aftertaste was sour.

If Oden's ankle wasn't troubling enough, the team's concerns multiplied when Conley began complaining of chest pains during the game. He was taken to the hospital as soon as it was over. At first doctors thought Conley was suffering from an asthma attack. But then doctors discovered an abnormality in his heart, forcing Conley to see a specialist. The short of it: Conley's status was in question for the next night's game against Decatur Central. It was yet another situation that summoned the ghost of John Stewart. Luckily, Conley went to see a cardiologist, who discovered that the membrane around Conley's heart was thicker than normal. It posed no health risk, and he was cleared to play.

However, Oden received no such clearance. He was still on the bench nursing his sore ankle when the Wildcats took the court against Decatur Central. Once again the team came out flat. Nothing seemed to be working, and the Wildcats were down by two at halftime. Coach Keefer put Oden into the starting line-up for the second half, and he sparked a charge in his teammates by scoring 10 points in limited playing time. The team was receiving a lift from another member, too. During the game, Coach Keefer watched Stefan Routt take his preseason chat to heart—and begin to play with a purpose. Routt lifted the team onto his back and led the Wildcats to victory with 16 points and 12 rebounds, as Lawrence North won 55-41.

Three days later came the showdown everyone had been waiting to see: Lawrence North versus the North Central Panthers. Fans packed into Southport High School, the tournament's neutral site, for what many thought would be the game of the year in the state of Indiana. North Central had a talented team with two future major college players, Tony Passley and A.J. Ratliff, who would later be named Mr. Basketball in Indiana for that season. The Panthers played a deliberate, slowdown offense, and on this day their shots were falling. With a little over three minutes left in regulation and Oden playing with four fouls, North Central hit a three-point shot to go up by one point. Lawrence North missed its next shot, and North Central's Ratliff hit a pair of free throws to make the score 41-38.

Routt was fouled and nailed both of his free throws to bring the Wildcats back to within one, but the Panthers scored inside and then stole the ball to retain possession. Ratliff hit Passley with a pass inside, and Oden fouled him as Passley made the basket. Passley leapt with joy. There were 95 seconds left, the Panthers were ahead, and Oden had just fouled out of the game. Passley hit his free throw to give North Central a commanding 46-40 lead.

But the Wildcats weren't in a quitting mood. Routt hit another free throw to draw the Wildcats to within five. That's when Conley stepped up to take over his first high school ballgame. Lawrence North put five guards into the game and pressed as the Panthers tried to bring the ball up the court. The Wildcats forced a turnover, and Conley banked in a three-point shot from the top of the key to make it a two-point game. On the ensuing possession, Conley stole the ball and fed Brandon McPherson, who was fouled on the drive to the hoop. McPherson sank his free throws to tie the game at 46-46.

Lawrence North forced yet another turnover on the next possession and called a time-out with 17 seconds left. Keefer told them to run a "line," a common in-bounds play that every team in the country runs some variation thereof. Four players line up in front of the player in-bounding the ball. One player darts right, another goes left, the third player turns to set a pick for the final player, who is hopefully freed of his defender to receive the pass and sink an easy, open shot. For the Wildcats, that fourth player was McPherson, even though he'd missed all six of his shot attempts in the game. He caught the ball and made a great move in the post to get to the basket, sink the shot, and put the Wildcats up by two.

The Panthers drove the ball upcourt with the clock ticking down. Conley deflected a last-second pass, and the Wildcat fans exploded in cheers. Passley, who thought he'd made the deciding play just 95 seconds earlier, slumped in a chair on his bench and stared at the scoreboard in disbelief: 48-46, Lawrence North. The Wildcats had scored eight straight unanswered points in 95 seconds to steal a victory.

It was the season's defining moment for the Wildcats. They had come back with Oden on the bench, which showed the team that even without their star 7-footer, they could win a game in the clutch. "I thought we were done," Coach Keefer said after the game. "The kids met the challenge. We're lucky to be alive."

Surviving the North Central game only strengthened Lawrence North's armor. They cruised past Warren Central for the second time that season to capture the Marion County Tournament championship, then blew out North Central on the Panthers' court, 86-62. With soaring confidence, the Wildcats dismissed Indianapolis Broad Ripple by 65 points, 120-55, then brushed aside four more teams like a cat pawing at a fly. One of those teams, Carmel, featured future Duke star Josh McRoberts; in that game, Conley scored 12 points, dished out 10 assists, and grabbed nine rebounds. But it was Sargent who led the Wildcats on the court with supreme confidence. Lawrence North was dictating the game's pace and playing on their terms.

But the air was sucked out of their collective swagger when the team traveled to face Bloomington South in mid-February. Their old nemesis—the stall—got the best of them again. The Wildcats lost 60-55 on Bloomington South's home court, and relinquished their No. 1 ranking. The game was a wake-up call for Lawrence North's players—and its staff. Coach Keefer determined that stall tactics would never again defeat his team. He knew he had to make an adjustment. His philosophy had always been to do whatever it took to get the other team out of their slowdown mode. His team would apply defensive pressure, chasing the other team all over the court while the minutes ticked away. Then Lawrence North would come down, get off a quick shot, and start chasing again. In the end, it just wore his players out.

Keefer decided that from now on, if a team slowed down the pace, so too would Lawrence North. Oden shot 70 percent from the field, and if the other team's intent was to minimize possessions, then Lawrence North would roll the dice and bank on their superior field-goal percentage to give them an edge. Their margin of victory might decrease, but it was better than taking a loss.

A week after the Bloomington South loss, the Wildcats hosted Pike, the new No. 1 team in the state. It was their first meeting since the de facto state championship showdown at the previous year's regionals at Hinkle Fieldhouse, which the Wildcats lost by eight points. In front of a standing-room-only crowd that exceeded 3,500 people, Oden had the best game of his young career, scoring 31 points, throwing down seven dunks, and grabbing 14 rebounds to lead Lawrence North to a 59-43 win. It was a big win—a statement to all opponents that the Wildcats' loss the previous week was a hiccup, not a trend.

For the final home game of the year against Terre Haute North, Coach Keefer benched Oden, Conley, and McPherson at the beginning of the game so that he could start an all-senior line-up. Terre Haute played a slowdown game and was behind by just three points late in the second quarter. But this time the Wildcats played smart and deliberate, slowing the tempo down to win 52-39.

In the first game of the state tournament sectionals, Lawrence North breezed past Indianapolis Manual, 73-35, setting up a game against the Irish of Indianapolis Cathedral. The game posed an interesting matchup for Oden against heralded freshman Keenan Ellis, who was 6-foot-10 but a rail-thin 170 pounds. Oden man-handled Ellis, scoring 26 points and hitting all 11 of his shots from the field to pace the Wildcats to a 74-51 win.

Oden's dominance caused Ellis to lose his cool. Walking off the court in the middle of the game, Ellis slapped away a water bottle offered up by the team manager. Later, he got into a fight in the locker room. Tempers often rage for opponents who suddenly find themselves helpless against Lawrence North; this was just another example of a rising star receiving a reality check compliments of Oden.

Arlington was up next in the sectional championship. Despite the presence of prolific scorer Fitzgerald Batteast, Arlington elected to ditch its usual game plan and slow down the game's tempo. The move shocked the Wildcats coaching staff, because Arlington was known for being a frenetic, in-your-face kind of team. When Arlington went into a five-out—putting all five players on the perimeter—and held the ball for the first minute of the game, the Lawrence North senior section began to chant, "You are scared! You are scared!" The stall tactic seemed to bother the Arlington players more than their counterparts. It was as if their coach had all but told them, "We can't beat them using our strength." Again, the Wildcats slowed their own pace down and took quality shots to seal another win over the Golden Knights, 61-47.

The win over Arlington set up a 10 a.m. matchup a week later between the Wildcats and Indianapolis Northwest in the regional semifinals at Hinkle Fieldhouse. The head coach at Northwest, Victor Bush, was a starting forward on Keefer's last state championship team in 1989, which also featured a dominating center, Eric Montross. After college, Bush had returned to Lawrence North to be a volunteer assistant coach. Keefer tried to get him a teaching job at the school, but Bush didn't get hired and wound up going to Warren Central before landing the Northwest job. Coach Keefer knew what to expect from his former player and understudy: in many ways, Bush was a junior version of himself. Bush's Northwest team had beaten Pike in the sectionals and was no pushover. But against Lawrence North, Bush just didn't have the players to stay in the game. The first half was close, but Lawrence North pulled away in the second half to win handily, 74-52.

Lawrence North's second game of the day was the matchup everyone had anticipated since the draws were announced: No. 1 Lawrence North against No. 2 North Central. As in last year's regional against Pike, this was viewed as the real state championship game, and a crowd of 6,100 turned out to watch. The question was which North Central team would show up: the team that took Lawrence North to the brink of defeat, or the one that had lost by 24 points?

For the Wildcats, it was an off night from the get-go. The team met at Coach Keefer's house and was late in leaving for the game. Then the bus got caught in traffic and by the time they reached the court at Hinkle, only 12 minutes remained for the team to warm-up before the opening tip. During the first half, both teams traded baskets, and as the half came to a close, the Wildcats clung to a slight 31-29 lead. In the second half, help came from an unexpected place. Tre Kemp, a seldom-used 6-foot-6 guard, came off the bench to hit two consecutive three-point shots and break the Wildcats out of their funk. Sargent led the team down the stretch as the Wildcats pulled away to win 66-53. After the game, Sargent wouldn't let his teammates celebrate. The goal was the state championship; winning the regional meant nothing more than advancing one step closer to the destination. "Go out and cut the nets down," he told the team. "Enjoy it. Then we've got more work to do."

Just two games separated Lawrence North from winning its first state championship since 1989. Standing in the way were the Bloomington North Cougars, perhaps the surprise of Indiana basketball with a 20-4 record. The game was held at Bedford North Lawrence High School, where Hoosier legend Damon Bailey had played high school ball. It was a 90-minute road trip for the Wildcats, yet only about 15 minutes away from Bloomington, which meant it would essentially be a home game for the Cougars in front of a standing-room-only crowd of more than 6,000 people.

The Cougars came out hot in the first half, hitting eight-of-12 three-point shots. Senior Anthony Lindsey alone hit four three-pointers, and the second quarter ended with the Cougars ahead 31-30. Bloomington North was employing a simple offensive strategy, running their perimeter shooters off of screens to get open looks. Lawrence North had never switched on outside "down picks," and didn't intend to give in now. But Coach Shelt saw the game slipping away and went down to Coach Scott, the team's defensive guru, and said, "We've got to switch. A guard-to-guard pick, you can switch. It's an equal switch."

Scott didn't take the suggestion well. "We don't switch down picks," he snapped back.

That got Shelt upset. "We're going to get our asses beat then." And he walked back to his seat.

At halftime, the two coaches smoothed things out and Coach Keefer made the change. "Bull on this," Keefer told himself. "We're switching. When a shooter's hitting like that, we've got to get out on him."

Keefer also had his players put on a full-court press that quickly turned the tide, suffocating the Cougars in the process. Lawrence North went on a 16-2 run in the third quarter, led by five points each from Sargent and Kemp. "I told our guys that if we kept playing hard, there was no way [Bloomington North] would hit like that in the second half," Sargent said after the game. "Then once we started running, I told the guys there was no way they would stay with us if we keep running."

Conley sunk the dagger in the Cougars' hearts at the start of the fourth quarter when he made a steal, hit a three-point shot, and laid in a shot off a rebound. Lindsey didn't score a single basket in the second half, and Bloomington North didn't hit another three. The Wildcats took the game 63-54; the championship was now one win away.

The days leading up to the state finals were dubbed Spirit Week at Lawrence North. Thousands of placards were printed up and posted in school windows or handed out. There was Army Day, where the student body collectively wore battle fatigues in support of the team. There was Red and Green Bahamas Day, where everyone wore Hawaiian shirts that reflected the Lawrence North colors. Classroom doors and lockers were decorated in green and red, and the school cheerleaders decorated the basketball team's school lockers. Kids even painted banners to hang along the highway route that would be taken by the school bus to the game at Conseco Fieldhouse in downtown Indianapolis.

All the hoopla was in anticipation of Lawrence North's second matchup of the season with the Columbia City Eagles, who had used the slowdown game to take the Wildcats to two overtimes earlier in the season. The Eagles were 25-3, ranked No. 6 in the state, and playing in their very first state finals in school history. They were paced by a twin-brother tandem at guard, Scott and Marcus Moore. Scott played the point and averaged 6.2 points a game, and his brother was the team's second leading scorer with 13.4 points a game. Columbia City played a three-guard offense; their primary inside presence was 6-foot-6 forward Doug Sheckler, who had averaged 15.5 points a game. Their other forward, Hugh Howard, was just 6-foot-2 and not much of an offensive threat.

Coach Keefer complained about Columbia City's deliberate style of offense to *The Indianapolis Star* in the build-up to the game. "It's not fun playing them because they'll put you on defense for 80 percent of the game," he said. "They'll spread the floor, pass the ball 10 or 12 times, and take the same shot on the 12th pass that they passed up on the fourth."

Complaining aside, Keefer knew his team would have a big advantage in terms of experience in pressure-packed games. Columbia City's schedule was hardly a match for Lawrence North's challenging run to the state finals. The Wildcats had played 18 top-25 teams that year; Columbia City had played just three. "Guys, it makes a difference who you play," he told the team. "If you can handle North Central and Pike, you can handle this."

And he truly believed that. The coaching staff had already devised what they thought was a foolproof game plan for Columbia City. For one, the Wildcats had already changed their approach to the slowdown game. When they had played Columbia City in late December, the Wildcats attacked the slowdown. They still ran fast breaks and swarmed on defense, and it had nearly cost them the game as the players grew frustrated and fatigued as the game progressed. Now the Wildcats were more patient against the slowdown, relying on Oden's presence and their high-percentage offense.

The coaches knew Sheckler and Marcus Moore were Columbia City's primary weapons. They would employ Sargent to shut down Moore, and use a team defense to aggressively attack the ball handler. "Put as much pressure on them as you can," Keefer told the team. "If you blow it, Greg will take care of you." The Wildcats were relying on Oden to take away the paint, intimidating any would-be scoring threats with his wingspan and shot-blocking ability. His mere presence would allow the Wildcats guards to pressure every pass, every drive, and every shot from the perimeter.

The Lawrence North coaches also knew that 6-foot-2 Hugh Howard really couldn't score. So they decided to have Oden guard him and to put Routt on Sheckler. The plan was for Routt to make Sheckler work for his buckets; if Sheckler drove around Routt, which he had to ability to do, then Oden would be there waiting.

Once again Routt would have to do the dirty work. But after his disastrous summer preparing for his senior season, he had blossomed thanks to his sit-down with Coach Keefer. Before the season started, the coaches told Routt that he'd be open a lot because his defender would probably be the one to double-down on Oden. And they reminded him that Oden was always looking to pass out before he looked for a shot. So Routt spent hours developing a mid-range jumper. After each practice, he would start 12 feet from the basket on the right baseline and shoot 50 jumpers. Then he'd take a few steps over and do it again. He'd perform the same routine on the left side of the court. When finished, he'd shoot free throws, and then repeat it all one more time. The results were easy to see: Routt had emerged as the team's second-leading scorer with 11.1 points a game and second-leading rebounder with 4.8 a game.

Keefer was supremely confident in his team, a point that was driven home in sound bytes that the press lapped up. He knew his game plan would work. But away from the cameras and tape recorders, Keefer was still working through emotions that had been bubbling near the surface for four seasons. Emotionally, Keefer was still haunted by the death of John Stewart. While his public face was rigid and strong, his private face betrayed him. His assistant coaches could tell something was bothering him, and wondered if the inner turmoil might be the team's undoing.

Then, the night before they took to the court for the title game, Keefer gathered his players and coaches together at half-court in the Lawrence North gymnasium. He brought out T-shirts sporting the number "53" and gave one to everyone. It was Stewart's number. Keefer refused to officially retire it, but Stewart's "53" jersey hung in the trophy case and no player since "Big John" had worn it.

Keefer had been put into an unenviable situation in the aftermath of Stewart's death. He wasn't allowed to mourn. Keefer had to be the strong father figure who held it together for everybody else—the team, the school, and the community. Jan Keefer, the coach's wife, told *The Indianapolis Star* that she thought her husband had repressed his feelings about the death. "He helped everyone through it," she said. "But he never has taken the time for himself to get through this."

Now it was as if he were at last laying himself bare, allowing the team to take on the role of caretaker. In a quiet, sometimes halting voice, he talked about Stewart as he never had before. He talked about the emotions. He talked about the feelings of helplessness. And he talked about the sense of loss. Everyone in the huddle was in tears, moved by the sudden vulnerability the coach was sharing with them. "Don't win for me and John," Keefer told them through his own tears. "Me and John, we'll work it out. You win for you."

There would be no late arrival this time around for Keefer's boys. The Wildcats bus left Lawrence on time, traveling to Conseco Fieldhouse with a full police escort. The players had never dealt with such hoopla before. Eyes wide open, they made their way to the home of the Indiana Pacers for the biggest day of their young athletic lives. A capacity crowd of 18,345 fans—many of who would view the class 1-A, 2-A, and 3-A finals in preparation for the main event, the 4-A final featuring Lawrence North—awaited them.

The Wildcats appeared cool and confident as they took to the court for their warm-ups, wearing their "53" T-shirts. Before the tip-off, Oden walked up to Coach Shelt, hugged him, and said, "Don't worry, Coach, we've got it." Conley had a similar thought in mind. The young guard approached Coach Etherington, patted him on the back and told him, "Sit down, Coach. We're going to win this—don't worry." If Etherington needed any additional boost to his confidence, he received it when he found a penny on the floor, heads up. Following his tradition, he picked it up, put it in his pocket, and told the other coaches, "John left that to let us know he's going to help out."

But Lawrence North hardly needed intervention. Oden blocked Columbia City's very first shot of the game. Sargent scored seven quick points—followed closely by five from Routt—as the Wildcats shot eight-of-nine from the field to bolt to a 19-2 lead. And when Routt and Sargent cooled off, Oden stepped up to score 11 out of the team's next 13 points. Early in the third quarter, Lawrence North went up 38-16, and the Eagles would never again be closer than 20 points. The Wildcats won going away, 50-29, and held the Eagles to the lowest scoring output in a state championship game since Washington beat Muncie Burris 24-18 in 1942. The Eagles shot just 27.5 percent, and 13.3 percent from beyond the three-point line.

Columbia City had no answer for the Wildcats' balanced offensive attack. "Are you going to get dunked on or give up the three?" Columbia City coach Chris Benedict asked rhetorically after the game. Graduating senior Penny Sargent paced his teammates with 11 points, topped only by Oden's 13. For Sargent, who had transferred to Lawrence North from Ben Davis after his freshman year only to endure the shocking 11-11 season as a sophomore, this win was sweet redemption. He was the team's leader, its heart and soul. As the team had grown, so too had he. When he got to Lawrence North, he had considerable problems dribbling to his left. So he stayed after practice to work with Coach Shelt, doing left-hand moves and learning to dribble efficiently with both hands. He also drastically improved his outside shot, until he was able to hit 25-foot jump shots with consistency by his senior year. His naysayers said he would never be a Division I collegiate player, but he proved them wrong by signing a scholarship with Bethune-Cookman College.

If something needed to be done, the coaches would say, "Sargent, do this," and it would be done. He was a no-nonsense kid, but he didn't lord over people; as a result, everybody liked him. He was the "glue guy," the team leader who held everyone together and refused to accept mediocrity. With his departure more of that responsibility would fall on Conley and Oden, as well as senior Brandon McPherson.

The final buzzer had barely sounded before people were talking about whether Lawrence North could repeat. Only a handful of Indiana high schools had ever done that. The Wildcats were losing Sargent and Routt to graduation, but they had able replacements waiting in the wings. The early consensus gave the Wildcats a strong chance to return to the championship stage in 2005.

"This year's team was very hungry," Coach Keefer would soon start saying. "Next year's team has to prove its hunger."

Coach Keefer kneels in front of his bench. Indiana High School Athletic Association, Inc.

SIX

N o one in his hometown could have predicted that John Robert Keefer was going to be a high school basketball coach, let alone one destined for the Indiana Basketball Hall of Fame. Born in the tiny, no-stoplight town of Sweetser, Indiana, in 1943, Keefer—who started going by Jack as a child—was the second of three children, sandwiched between two girls. His parents, Dale and Maradell, divorced when he was in fourth grade due to his father's alcoholism. Dale used to take Keefer and his two sisters, Jill and Ann, to the tavern and leave them sitting in the car while he drank inside. It was hardly an ideal way to spend a night, but the kids hung together.

Keefer's young childhood may best be summed up by one incident in particular: His grandfather had a habit of opening the car door—while he was driving—to spit out his tobacco juice onto the road. Young Keefer took notice, and one day followed suit, opening his backseat passenger door to spit. Leaning out the door, he tumbled out of the car and landed in the middle of a gravel road. Fortunately, the car was only going about 15 miles per hour, so Keefer was not seriously injured. His family hadn't realized he had fallen out until Keefer caught up with the car on a dead sprint.

Life was anything but easy for little Keefer. His mother worked long hours at the RCA plant six miles down the road in Marion to support her children. Times were tight, and from a young age Keefer realized he had to do his share of work if he ever wanted to have anything for himself. Not long after his parents' divorce, he began to earn money by mowing lawns. He also worked in the school cafeteria to pay for his lunch, and spent his summers at work, holding down various jobs including a stint at a tomato plant.

Keefer saw very little of his father following his parents' divorce. But his old man started his 11-year-old son down a career path when he erected an old telephone pole in the yard and placed a basket atop it. Thus began Keefer's love affair with basketball. But the affair turned sour the following year, when in seventh grade Keefer was cut from the junior high basketball team in his first crack at playing organized ball. An older neighbor, Mick Wilson, rallied Keefer's spirits, working with him day after day on a backyard cement court. The following year, Keefer made the squad.

In high school—first at Sweetser High and later at Oak Hill, which formed after Sweetser consolidated with nearby Converse High— Keefer played football, basketball, baseball, and ran track, graduating in 1961 with 13 letters to his credit. On the basketball court he played second fiddle to 6-foot-8 teammate Earl Brown, who earned a scholarship to Purdue University. Keefer was noted for his hustle, strong work ethic, and rebounding skills, which helped him overcome a lack of natural ability.

During his junior season, Oak Hill defeated powerhouse Marion during the state playoffs in a come-from-behind thriller—capped by Keefer's lone basket, a 15-foot game-winner—and eventually captured the sectional crown. As a 6-foot-1 senior forward, Keefer became a starter and again was a thorn in the side of favored Marion. Keefer poured in 17 points as Marion fell to Oak Hill in the state playoffs for the second consecutive year, this time by a much more resounding 69-52 margin. Oak Hill went on to again win the sectional crown. Over his final two high school seasons, Oak Hill went 41-9.

Away from the court, Keefer continued to display the orneriness that marked his childhood. In typing class he tied a string to his textbook and threw it out of a three-story window, much to his teacher's dismay. His teacher got over her shock quickly, though, when he pulled the book back up through the window moments later.

Keefer would sneak out of the house and hitchhike into Marion with his buddies to play pool or poker. Later he inherited his grandfather's car, a two-door 1948 Chevy, which Keefer repaired and repainted, christening it, affectionately, the "Blue Bitch." He was one of the few teenagers in town who had a car, and he proudly drove it to school each day, even though he lived a mere two blocks away.

During his sophomore year, Keefer's mischievousness was curbed when the principal called him into his office and threatened to kick him out of school if he didn't shape up. The wake-up call did the trick, and Keefer began to show a sensitive side in school. He authored a paper expressing how painful it was to be without a father. The lack of a father figure plagued Keefer throughout his youth, and eventually may have helped steer him into coaching, where he has been able to make a positive impact on the lives of teenagers.

Growing up, Keefer noted that the most respected people he knew were either teachers or ministers. He attended the Sweetser Methodist Church and even went to church camp, which to him was a big deal. Today he calls himself "religious but not one that puts it on my sleeve." Apparently he ruled out becoming a minister, because he decided to attend Ball State University and major in business with a minor in physical education. If business did not work out, Keefer planned to fall back on coaching or teaching. Still, he had no great desire to coach at this point in his life, because as he puts it, "I wasn't a deep planner." Yet he had the foresight to find construction work the summer after his graduation from high school, so that he could save up enough money to afford college tuition.

Money in hand to pay for his schooling, Keefer looked forward to his first semester in college. He tried out for, and made, the freshman Ball State basketball team. But he was cut during varsity tryouts as a sophomore because he was not tall enough to play inside and didn't handle the ball well enough to play guard. However, he excelled in his four-year career as a high hurdler in track. Even though the college hurdles were three inches taller than in high school, he improved his best time from 15.7 seconds in high school to 15.2 seconds at BSU thanks to that old standby, determination.

Hard work was a staple of Keefer's college years. When not in class, he was busy earning money as a cafeteria worker, a clothing store employee, and a driver for a dog and cat food supply business, in addition to construction work. Keefer also launched what was to become a very lucrative side career in real estate when he and roommate Jim Taylor bought a 13-room house in Muncie, and rented out rooms to members of their fraternity, Lambda Chi. The money they made from collecting rent allowed them to live there rent free. Hustling for every penny, Keefer basically worked his way through college. Until his senior year, he never had to take out a student loan.

After graduating from Ball State in 1965, Keefer married his high school sweetheart, Sue Sirk, and took a job teaching at Frankfort (Indiana) High School, which offered one of the state's highest paying positions for first-year teachers. His salary was a handsome $5,700. The following spring, Keefer was asked to return to his alma mater, Oak Hill, as head track coach and freshman basketball coach. He wound up coaching track for 10 years and was named head basketball coach for his final four years. As head coach of the basketball team, Keefer compiled a 61-26 record from 1972-76. While serving as an assistant under head basketball coach Galen Smith, Keefer helped coach mighty mite Monte Towe, who later starred with David Thompson on North Carolina State's 1974 NCAA championship team.

During his Oak Hill tenure, Keefer received his first taste of coaching a family member. His brother-in-law, Flava Sirk, was on the team, and soon Keefer found himself incurring the wrath of his father-in-law, Bob Sirk, by not starting Flava as a junior. Keefer stood his ground, refusing to show favoritism. Keefer was Flava's idol, but the youngster rode the pine for the first five games of the season—four of them losses. Bob Sirk left the gym following a loss, muttering, "I hope Keefer loses every game!" Keefer finally inserted Flava into the starting five for the sixth game, and Flava was first team the rest of his career. Keefer's message, however, was clear: a player earned his way into the starting lineup. There were no free passes, even for family.

As a young coach, Keefer began to display many of the peculiarities that would give him character as a veteran many years later. Keefer developed an interesting superstition while coaching at Oak Hill: He had to bring the same old pen to every basketball game. Once, having forgotten the pen at home, he called Sue and asked her to quickly bring it to the game. Without his pen—which Sue later learned was dry of ink—he was doomed.

Oak Hill athletic trainer Steve Fagan, who sat on the team bench, saw many qualities develop within Keefer that have made him a winning coach. He spent countless hours every summer working with kids to develop their full potential, and he always gave his assistant coaches great responsibility. He was a consistent disciplinarian who demanded that his players learn the fundamentals. On the court, he was an intense competitor, and he expected the same from his players. Should they fail, he was quick to remind them. At halftime of a sectional game, Keefer yelled so intensely at his players that his bridge—two false teeth—flew out of his mouth, landing several feet away.

Keefer's bitterest loss at Oak Hill was a 48-46 heartbreaker against hated rival Marion in the sectional tournament. The Golden Eagles were up four points with just over a minute left. Marion tied the score, then as Oak Hill was working for the winning shot, the referee under the basket blew his whistle to surprisingly signal a three-second violation. The turnover gave the ball back to Marion, who wound up winning the game. Marion principal Dick Persinger told Keefer several years later that he had hollered "three seconds" at the referee, and he believes the official made the call strictly as a reflex. Apparently, no Oak Hill player had been in the lane and, therefore, no violation should have been called.

Keefer stewed over the missed opportunity. He believed he was in line to become head coach at a new school being built in Indianapolis, and he fretted that he had just blown his big chance to land the job thanks to that loss in the state tournament. He had a great team that year, but the handwriting was on the wall: if he wanted to win a state championship he really needed to break free from the shadows of perennial powerhouse Marion, who would go on to win back-to-back titles.

It turned out that Oak Hill's gut-wrenching loss to Marion bore two positives for Keefer: His efforts in that game impressed his coaching peers—who soon began calling him for advice on how to beat Marion—as well as representatives at that new Indianapolis school, Lawrence North High School. Keefer was offered that coaching gig—as well as another. Bloomington South, which was coming off an uncharacteristic 2-20 season, also inquired about Keefer's services. It took him only a few moments, though, to realize that Indiana University and its flamboyant coach, Bobby Knight, would always rule in Bloomington. He had a much better chance to build his own "kingdom" from scratch in suburban Indianapolis.

Lawrence North started with 1,100 students (no seniors) in 1976, a far cry from the 3,000 students it would have 30 years later. Keefer realized starting over at a new school was a gamble of sorts, especially with no senior class. His nervousness increased when school officials told him that he had a quarterback to play forward, a fullback at guard or forward, and a tackle at center. He quickly asked, "Do you have any *basketball* players here?"

To build his program, the new coach sought out athletes first, with quickness at the top of his list. In the high-octane offense and defense he was about to install, speed was a necessary trait. A positive attitude, compassion, and desire were the intangibles he highly valued. Those qualities, he believed, would translate into competitiveness and a powerful drive to accept nothing but victory. This all-out attitude has been embodied in many of Keefer's protégés over the years, but probably never more so than in All-State guard Todd Leary, who helped the Wildcats win their first state championship in 1989.

"The thing I got from [Coach Keefer] more than anything else is how much it sucked to lose," says Leary. "You could tell it ruined his whole life when he lost."

As for other basketball skills—ball handling, shooting, passing, defense—Keefer could teach those things in practice. What he couldn't teach was height. He is a firm believer in putting together the tallest team possible, which often means taking on "projects," players who may have ideal basketball bodies but lack basketball skill and acumen. Such projects require a coach to spend lots of hours with young, awkward teens who are still growing while attempting to learn the game. Some coaches don't have the patience or the will to work with big, raw players, instead allowing them to languish on the bench and never reach their full potential. But Keefer has always welcomed the challenge.

He decided that Lawrence North would employ one of the most intense defenses in the Hoosier state—a full-court, pressing defense. Keefer's practices would continually be based on improving an already intense defensive effort. Former 7-foot Lawrence North standout Eric Montross, who later enjoyed a 10-year career in the NBA, recalls being "gassed" after Keefer's practice sessions. "Defense Wins" was stamped on his players' shorts and T-shirts, in the locker room, and in the gym. Keefer breathed defense like most people suck in oxygen, and his players had no choice but to follow suit.

To be able to keep his players fresh while they apply constant pressure on defense, Keefer rotates his bench players in and out of games, which also helps them maintain a sense of importance. For Keefer, the key to success at his new program would be defense—and the key to a great defense was a deep rotation of players, all of who have to buy into the team concept.

Keefer spends time developing each player's athleticism as well as his fundamentals. He requires all of his players to participate in weight training, which works toward the goal of improving agility and quickness, saving the coaches time in practice to focus on issues of basketball IQ as well as determination. Keefer develops toughness and discipline in his players through a series of practice drills. He stresses that the aggressor sets the game's tempo. A 5-on-5 rebound drill quite aptly named "war" can become quite physical. If the offensive team secures the rebound, the defensive players have to run. If his players don't dive for loose balls during the drill, the players again have to run. Stefan Routt, a bright kid and talented player, will never forget the fistfights that used to erupt during practice due to players arguing amongst each other as a result of running laps. Routt would come home from practice with cuts and bruises, but still insists the experience was beneficial. He maintains that he has never met anyone who loved basketball as much as Keefer, and he has the utmost respect for him. The pain of being pushed to his physical limit was worth all the lessons he learned.

But the wise coach does realize that some drills have limits best not broken. Another drill he employs forces players to dive on the floor for a loose ball. But Keefer doesn't use it too often due to the injuries that often result. "I want my players to *think* they impress me by drawing blood," he says matter of factly.

Keefer's intensity struck hard at freshman guard Mike Conley, who readily admitted he wasn't accustomed to being yelled at like that by a coach. Greg Oden was also shaken a few times as a freshman, but he realized early on that the veteran coach "always teaches you something new and always pushes you to the limit." If one of his players gets a big head, Keefer reserves a special place for him—at the far end of the bench. The last thing he wants to hear from a player is an excuse when something goes wrong. Despite the program's intensity, Keefer does allow Wildcat practices to taper off somewhat as the season progresses, especially following the big Marion County Tournament in mid-January, so his players can be fresh for the sectional tournament. Keefer adopted the philosophy of a gradual decline from University of Texas men's basketball coach Rick Barnes, who had relayed a story from his own swim coach. Upon watching Barnes' squad compete, the swim coach told him that he pushed his players so hard in practice that they were "dead-legged and tired" for the start of the NCAA basketball tourney each year.

Even an old dog like Keefer is open to learning new tricks. If it's good for his team, he will take the advice.

There are no "yes men" serving under Keefer. Knockdown, drag-out arguments are typical amongst Keefer and his coaching staff—concerning everything from roster cuts to in-game decisions. The conflict is by design. Keefer's shrewdness in selecting assistant coaches equals his passion for assembling the best roster of players. He desires an intelligent, confident coaching staff, but also a staff with impeccable character. He searches for family men, individuals who have a love for the game, and then he bestows upon them massive responsibility. That trust keeps his assistants content and by his side for many years, even though head-coaching job offers wait in the wings. This provides the Lawrence North program with a knowledgeable, stable staff and gives Keefer his rock to lean upon.

Longtime assistant Ralph Scott is in charge of the Wildcat big men and team defense, while Jim Etherington handles advance scouting and the teaching of zone defense, in addition to keeping tabs on the players' academic standing. (The team has produced the winner of the state's coveted Class 4A Trester Award—based on grades and mental attitude—for an unprecedented three straight years beginning in 2004.) Joe Leonard handles the team's press defense, and J.R. Shelt develops set offensive plays and works on timing factors. (Shelt followed in Coach Keefer's footsteps in the summer of 2006 when he accepted a head coaching position at the newly launched Fishers High School in suburban Indianapolis.)

The assistants receive no shortcuts, just like the players. In addition to participating in regular afternoon practices, they also host individual workouts at 6 a.m. four days a week during the season, and open gyms twice a week during the spring and three times per week during the summer. Keefer attends all open gym sessions as well. He's demanding of his assistants but holds himself to the same standard.

To a man, Keefer's assistants swear by him. Scott concedes that the coach's incredible work ethic has "rubbed off" on the entire staff. Etherington loves Keefer's fanaticism for both work and fun—a difficult balance that he successfully strikes. Somehow Keefer drains every ounce of ability out of his players without destroying their joy for the game. For accomplishing this feat, Keefer has been described as a "pied piper."

Perhaps Leonard best paints a picture of why Keefer is so loved by his assistants. In the summer of 2004, Leonard took the school's junior varsity team to the Indiana University team camp in Bloomington, while Keefer oversaw the varsity squad at the same camp. The junior varsity team lost two lopsided games on the first day of camp, and Leonard's players were so out of control that he even had to break up a fight on his own bench. He described the team as "12 loose cannons." Utterly discouraged, Leonard told Keefer that night that he was quitting. The next morning, however, Keefer got on the junior varsity bus and began opening up to the players, sharing stories of the tough life he had endured as a young boy. Later that day Leonard's junior varsity players rallied to win three games—including two defeats of teams that had routed them the previous day—to capture the junior varsity camp championship. By the camp's completion, Leonard could hardly wait for the next season to start, and his players had regained their focus.

When it comes to dealing with youth, motivation is an asset a successful high school coach cannot do without. Keefer motivates his younger players in much the same fashion as his varsity players. The junior varsity team often practices with and against the varsity team, which serves to bond the two units, but also helps in developing the younger players at a faster pace by significantly improving their competition day in and day out. Keefer says with confidence that his junior varsity players are often better than the players on some opposing varsity teams. Numerous others have echoed this sentiment. Penny Sargent, whose toughness and leadership rubbed off on his teammates, is certain that the varsity squad lost more games to the junior varsity team in practices than it did to outsiders in actual competition.

Keefer's marriage to high school sweetheart Sue Sirk ended in divorce after 15 years when their only son, Joel, was in first grade. Joel lived with his mother, who had remarried but shared custody with Jack. Joel saw plenty of his father growing up, and by his own admission, basketball was all the youngster cared about. He would spend Friday and Saturday nights and entire summer evenings in the Lawrence North gym. Sue later moved into the Lawrence North district so that Joel could play ball for his dad. Under the tutelage of his father, Joel became an outstanding 6-foot-1 shooting guard. He broke into the starting lineup during the last half of his sophomore year in 1991, and set a school record as a junior by drilling seven three-pointers in a single half.

Heading into his senior season, Joel had high expectations for landing an NCAA Division I basketball scholarship. However, he hit a major speed bump on the road to that scholarship: the truth. Growing up, he had dreams of playing for a national powerhouse like the University of North Carolina, just like former Wildcat Eric Montross. As reality began to set in, he lowered his sights to a mid-major school such as Butler, before finally becoming disheartened when no Division I scholarships were forthcoming.

Joel was a shooter, but he admits to being "slow as molasses" and unable to put on weight. He was a very sensitive teenager and wanted more out of himself than he could give. In the final analysis, he probably was somewhat burned out from years of allowing basketball to dominate his life. As his son's interest in playing ball waned, Keefer appealed to him, pointing out that he was the team's best shooter.

But the motivational plea—even from his father—was simply not enough. Joel quit the game he had worshipped his entire life at the zenith of his high school career. Instead of playing for his dad his senior year, Joel became co-editor of the school newspaper and acted in a school play. He says he will never forget the "ultra-classy" way his father handled the situation. He is proud to note that Keefer attended his play and supported all of his extracurricular activities. It was a caring move for someone caught in an awkward situation. After all, what coach would be happy about losing his team's best shooter?

"I loved coaching him," Keefer says of Joel, now a teacher and a coach himself, "but at the same time it was hard" because of outside criticism that comes with the territory of any father-son coaching relationship. The bottom line: Keefer just wanted his son to be happy. So Keefer Keefer the coach gracefully accepted the loss on behalf of Keefer Keefer the father.

Keefer married the former Jan Kepley in June of 1984. The oldest of five girls, Jan grew up in Bowie, Maryland, but graduated from Marion High School where she was a varsity swimmer and grew to love basketball thanks to her father. She later graduated from Indiana University's law school and now practices family law in Indianapolis.

Jan adds to the family atmosphere that her husband cultivates with his players. She coordinates many team dinners at their home, and like Keefer truly loves being around the players. She rarely, if ever, misses a game. Keefer calls his wife a "special lady— very sharp and insightful." She never fails to remind him that he did not win a sectional title until he met her.

In the summer of 1997, they adopted a newborn son, Jake, who his parents describe as a mini ball of fire. Jake is a fixture at every Lawrence North basketball game, moving with ease from the bench to the bleachers and even into press row. Jake has given the silver-haired coach yet another reason to take it all in stride. Possibly, the youngster will continue to keep Keefer, now in his 60s, young at heart as well. Jan would love to see Keefer coach their son when he reaches high school age. Keefer puts things into sharper focus when he says, simply, that coaching is "better than being a greeter at Wal-Mart." That much is true, at least for Keefer.

By the end of the 2005-06 basketball season, Keefer had amassed 583 wins in his career, against just 227 losses. But Keefer didn't trail blaze the path to such an overwhelming record overnight. Actually, it took him a day or two. Beginning his first season at Lawrence North in 1976-77 with no seniors on the roster, Keefer's Wildcats struggled to an 8-13 mark. However, the following year he turned his team's fortunes around with a 22-2 mark. The Wildcats won their first 19 games that year—including the prestigious Marion County Tournament title—until being upset by Lapel High School. They later lost in the sectional to Indianapolis Cathedral.

Still not satisfied with his team's development, Keefer revamped a weak schedule into one of the state's most intimidating, setting up games with every strong team he could fit into the schedule in order to prepare his team for the pressures of the state tournament. The results were astounding, especially for a high school just out of the gate: Keefer guided the Wildcats to championships in the Central Suburban Athletic Conference in 1979, 1981, and 1983, and in 1980 his Wildcats won the prestigious Hall of Fame Tournament. Keefer culminated his efforts in the 1984-85 season by winning the first of 14 sectional titles and the first of six regional titles at Lawrence North. That group would hardly resemble the sort of team he would field in the future. No player on the 1984-85 team stood taller that 6-foot-3. Each had grown up attending Keefer's summer basketball camp, and each resembled their coach in their ability to overachieve. Senior guard Reed Crafton became his first of many Indiana All-Stars.

The following year Keefer suffered his third losing season at Lawrence North. But the season was but a small misstep for Keefer's program. Within three years, Lawrence North would reach the pinnacle—their first state championship. With a 25-4 record and a glittering No. 13 ranking in the country bestowed by *USA Today*, Keefer's 1988-89 team became the first Marion County suburban school to turn the trick.

Hopes remained high the following year with 7-foot All-American Eric Montross returning from the state champion team. In the first round of the regional, the Wildcats nipped No. 3-ranked Pike in a true heart-stopper, 69-68, before 9,000 fans at Hinkle Fieldhouse. The Red Devils, who had beaten the Wildcats twice during the regular season, held a one-point lead with less than 30 seconds to play. Keefer called for his players to foul, and Damon Watts obliged by hitting Jason Williams on the arm. The players for both teams stopped in their tracks, assuming that a foul had been called. But the referee never blew his whistle, so Wildcat Keith Berryhill alertly scooped up the loose ball and drilled a 15-foot jump shot with 21 seconds left to give Lawrence North the lead. Pike missed on its final shot attempt, and one of the greatest games in Indianapolis history went into the record books, odd finish and all.

Eight future Division I recruits and four Indiana All-Stars were on the court that day for Pike and Lawrence North. But Montross stole the show for the Wildcats with 32 points (16-of-20 shooting from the field) and 19 rebounds. Pike's standout 6-foot-9 center, Marcus Johnson, countered with 27 points. The teams combined for an impressive 31 assists and just 23 turnovers. There were five ties and 20 lead changes in the frenzied 32-minute contest.

Pike coach Ed Siegel refused to protest the game's ending sequence, because he didn't want to diminish what he felt had been a classic match between two spectacular teams. His feelings were validated afterward by University of North Carolina coach Dean Smith, who approached the coaches to congratulate them. Present to watch his future recruit, Montross, Smith said he had just witnessed a game played far above the high school level. He called it "two guys playing checkers" and "an absolute coaching clinic." He told both coaches that he had never witnessed a high school game with so much intensity and desire.

Indianapolis News sports editor Wayne Fuson also thanked Siegel and Keefer for raising Indianapolis basketball to a higher level. He wrote that the thriller "was one of the all-time epic high school basketball games in the history of Hinkle Fieldhouse"—a high compliment considering the cavernous barn had been home to many state championship games over the years.

Unfortunately, after experiencing such an emotional high, the Wildcats had to return that same night for the regional title game, and were upset by Southport, a team they had beaten by 15 points during the regular season. Keefer believes that his team had the talent to win its second title that year, which might have enabled Montross to be named Mr. Basketball over Damon Bailey of Bedford North Lawrence. Losing to Southport remains one of his greatest disappointments.

In 1993, another Keefer big man, 6-foot-9 Jeff Leyden, earned Indiana All-Star honors. He says candidly that playing for Keefer was at times "pure hell," elaborating that "there were days you just wanted to cry." Now that he is a coach, Leyden looks upon Keefer in a completely different light, however, realizing what a great motivator he was. "All of his [ex-] players absolutely love him."

In 1997, 6-foot-7, 255-pound Tom Geyer joined Keefer's distinguished list of Indiana All-Stars. He notes that his years under Keefer made his transition to Indiana University and coach Bob Knight much easier than the experiences of his college teammates. Keefer had done an excellent job of preparing Geyer for life on and off the college court. Geyer notes that both Coach Knight and Coach Keefer are most concerned with how their players turn out in life, and therefore they greet a steady flow of ex-players who return each year to visit them.

Keefer's players would probably suggest the great rapport they share with their coach as a big reason for Lawrence North's continued success. But the veteran coach defers some of the credit of his team's success to the atmosphere of their gymnasium, rather than the atmosphere of their huddle. In a state containing most of the nation's largest high school gyms, Lawrence North's gym seats a mere 3,500 fans. Yet Keefer loves the vocal enthusiasm displayed in his "cracker box," and the fact that fans must arrive early to get a seat.

Possibly it's that rush of adrenaline he gets every time he steps into his cracker box that has kept Keefer at it so long. He is the first to confess that he didn't expect to be coaching this long. He anticipated a career in real estate would have lured him away from coaching by this point in his life. But he still loves to coach, even though he laments that it's not the same since Indiana abandoned its famous one-class system in the 1997-98 school year. He has seen once-heated rivalries between small and large schools weaken greatly, and overall interest decline throughout the state. He believes the change to a four-class system "has killed the spirit" for many fans.

Just not his.

Greg Oden is interviewed by ESPN announcer Jay Williams. Photo by David Dixon

SEVEN

After averaging 14 points and 10 rebounds a game as a sophomore, Greg Oden's world changed. He was an agile and athletic 7-footer entering his junior season, and with his team primed to make another run at Indiana's state title, he had all the experts abuzz. The nation's top three recruiting experts were already saying it was a near certainty that he would be the No. 1 pick in the 2006 NBA draft if he decided to turn pro after his senior year of high school. Some took the praise a step further, claiming that if Oden would have been allowed to turn pro after his sophomore season, he *still* would have been selected with the NBA's top draft pick. With a landscape populated by precious few dominant big men, the NBA was lusting after Oden.

If Oden did decide to jump to the pros straight from high school, he would become an instant multimillionaire, banking on a guaranteed contract of approximately $20 million for four years, plus tens of millions more in endorsement money. LeBron James, who was the No. 1 pick when Oden was a high school freshman, was estimated to have brought home $250 million in salary and endorsements during his first year in the league. It was heady stuff for a 16-year-old who had yet to obtain his driver's license and was living a modest life in a two-bedroom apartment with his family. The "next big thing" was a world away from the glitz and glamour of the NBA. He still had to share a bedroom with his younger brother Anthony, who was 6-foot-8, 260 pounds and still growing.

Despite their hulking frames, the two brothers were like night and day. Their personalities were so different. Anthony was into hip-hop culture, loud and outgoing; Greg was reserved, very much a youthful adult. On occasion, Lawrence North coaches would laugh at the thought of how the two behemoths could share a room and not share at least *some* conversation. But the two did not have a talkative relationship.

Still, they were family, and no one doubted their loyalty to one another. They spoke to each other, but on their own terms. Greg showed up one day with a tattoo on his left shoulder that read, "Always there." When the coaches asked him about it, he replied, "I got it for my brother." It was a message from one to the other: No matter what, I've got your back.

The tattoo was a bold move for Greg, who was quiet by nature. He wasn't fond of all the attention he was receiving; in an ideal world, he'd rather slip on headphones and slink into the background. At school he was a good student, maintaining a high B average. His favorite subject was math, and he was leaning toward a business major in college. That's right: college. Though no one believed him, Oden insisted he would go to college and rebel against what many thought was a no-brainer in entering the NBA draft at first chance. No matter what the scouts said, Oden felt he was far from being NBA ready, and didn't want to compete against the world's best players until he was ready to truly *earn* the big bucks he stood to make.

Oden was out of step with accepted logic in terms of his post-high school desires, and he was also still adjusting socially to teenage life. Even though he was a star in a basketball-hungry state, he found fitting in with his classmates to be somewhat of a challenge. It was especially hard in junior high before the fame arrived, when he was at an age where anything that made you stand out from your peers also made you feel very awkward. There was no way for him to hide the thing that made him different: his size. Oden stood a good foot above his male classmates, a differential that was only exaggerated when it came to girls. As a defensive mechanism, Oden developed a shield against the world. He would cut loose when he was with friends he felt comfortable with, but he was reserved—yet polite—with people he didn't know well.

The basketball court was his refuge—the one place where his size wasn't perceived as awkward, rather as a blessing. On the court, his companion at all times was Mike Conley. The two had played together since the sixth grade, so they were as tight as brothers by their junior year of high school. They had developed an inherent and deep trust from battles fought together and won. They didn't always hang out together away from the court. But whenever one of them needed the other, they were there for each other.

The relationship wouldn't have worked—either off the court and especially on the court—if Conley had fostered any hidden jealousy of Oden's fame. Instead, he took pride in being Greg's superb sidekick. Conley was to Oden what Scottie Pippen had been to Michael Jordan—the ultimate complement on the court. "Greg gets a lot of the press and a lot of attention, but that doesn't bother me," Conley said. "I just take advantage of the opportunities I get, play my game, and play my hardest. I know if I do that, people will notice me. And if people come to games to see Greg, then they'll see me, too."

Conley's parents had been a deep influence on each of them. Mike Conley Sr. was familiar with fame, having won an Olympic gold medal. He was used to people always wanting to be in his business, and so he'd learned to keep to himself and a tight circle of friends. He was picky about the people he invited into his family. He didn't teach Greg and Mike to be cautious of people, but he did teach them to be guarded in what they said and in what they did.

Such lessons aided Conley and Oden in becoming mature for their age. Their maturity was evident in the way they carried themselves, and it went with them onto the court. Though both were blessed with natural talent, they hungered to improve and were willing to make sacrifices and put in the work necessary to do it. Whatever it took: early-morning practices became a part of their daily routine. No excuses were accepted.

In June, Oden and Conley went to Richmond, Virginia, to the National Basketball Players Association Top 100 camp—where the country's brightest prep stars gathered—and Oden was the hit of the party. "I use two words to describe him: major star," Tim McCormick, a former NBA center who had directed the camp all 10 years of its existence, told *The Indianapolis Star*. It would have been easy for Conley to get lost in Oden's shadow, but he also made a strong impression at the camp. Conley had averaged 9.6 points his sophomore season, with 4.7 assists, 3.7 rebounds, and three steals per game. He had the perfect point guard mentality because he relished setting up his teammates, but he also had the talent to step up his own offensive game when the team needed it. The camp allowed him to compete against the caliber of guards he didn't often see in Indiana. Conley held his own against the nation's top talent, and he left the camp being touted as one of the top-five point guards of his high school class. His stock with college coaches grew; if they couldn't get Greg Oden, Mike Conley was an excellent consolation prize.

Both Conley and Oden played AAU ball throughout the summer in addition to showing up at the open gyms at Lawrence North. In May, their Spiece Indy Heat AAU team—coached by Conley Sr. and also featuring Carmel's Josh McRoberts and North Central's budding star Eric Gordon—won the Reebok/Bob Gibbons Tournament of Champions. Then in July, they traveled to Las Vegas to win the Reebok Big Time Tournament. In the championship game, Oden scored 26 points, with 14 rebounds and five blocked shots, and was named the tournament's Most Outstanding Player.

Despite the hoopla and attention, neither one of them were looking past their junior year of high school and the chance to earn a second straight state championship. "We would love to repeat next year," Conley said. "Few teams have done it, and we have the talent and are a good enough team to do it. Everyone on the team has been working hard to improve. We want to be the team with the target on our back."

Coach Keefer liked to share the following anecdote with his players: A grandfather had worked hard to build a business and get it to the point that it was very successful. When his son took over, he'd watched his father work his rear off and spend all those long hours on the job. He appreciated what his father had accomplished, but had no hunger in his belly to work quite that hard. Still, he did what was required to keep the business successful, maybe even grow it. But when the grandson took over, he was too far removed from the business' origin. He'd never witnessed his grandfather's work ethic to build the business. He didn't have the same appreciation for hard work as his father because he'd already lived a life where everything had been given to him—thanks to the labor of those who came before him. So when the third generation took over the business, it started to fail.

"Do you want to be that third generation?" Keefer would ask his players. "Two years ago, we had success. Last year, we won the state championship. This is the third year. Do you want to be the kind of team that doesn't achieve all that it can?"

The players all received T-shirts that read, "Defending The Legacy." Keefer hammered home the point that nothing was guaranteed. "What do you want to be known for?" he asked. "In 20 years, when people look back, how do you want them to view you?" With that, he let the message soak in: Do not take success for granted. Put in the same hard work as usual, and stay focused on the goal—another championship.

Just before the season began, Coach Keefer met with the members of last year's team and continued to hammer his themes, questioning whether they were still hungry. "My wife said she noticed how you all have grown up. You're not kids anymore. What do you do now that you are not fighting for respect?"

One of Keefer's chief tasks heading into the 2004-05 season was to keep the distractions at bay. Lawrence North was scheduled to play on national television against Missouri's Poplar Bluff High School. Magazines and media—from *Sports Illustrated* to ESPN—lined up to interview Oden for features. *Indianapolis Monthly's* Tony Rehagan even went to class with him to pen a feature with a unique twist. During one open-gym session leading up to the early December game, 20-some college coaches huddled up in the Lawrence North gym to get a peek at Oden and his teammates. Some of them were becoming more optimistic that they could recruit Oden, first to college in general, and second to their school in specific. He was, after all, proclaiming his desire to go to college just as the NBA was beginning to discuss the idea of excluding high school players from their annual draft, forcing them into at least one year of college or prep school.

At that point, Conley and Oden were privately favoring Michigan State because former Wildcats star Chris Hill was currently playing there, and the duo were friends with him. But then Michigan State inexplicably stopped recruiting them. One coach who did want them was Thad Matta. He was a Hoosier and had been an assistant coach at his alma mater, Butler University, before he moved on to be head coach at Xavier University. Matta was at Xavier University when he first started to show interest in both Oden and Conley, even though he knew Xavier was likely too small a school to really compete for star talent with big-time programs.

But in 2004, after taking Xavier to the Elite Eight in the NCAA tournament, Matta pounced on an opportunity to jump ship to Ohio State. And all of a sudden, he found himself on the inside track for the two high school players he held most dear.

The first official day of practice for the Lawrence North 2004-05 season was November 8. The coaches were excited and so were the players … at least the ones on the court. Three seniors nonchalantly joined the team late: Warren Wallace, Korey Bobo, and Brandon Coffer. And that was only the third thing to go wrong in the first 10 minutes of practice. First, Donald Cloutier came out wearing blue shorts and a grey T-shirt instead of the red-and-green Lawrence North colors. Then Anthony Oden, Greg's younger brother and a freshman, walked out on the court with his hair done up in corn-rows, even though he knew Coach Keefer had a longstanding, strict dress code and did not accept flashy hairstyles. Finally, Zach Stewart, another senior, suggested a little too loudly, "We should just have open gym until we play Lawrence Central," insinuating that the team didn't need to do much to prepare for the upcoming season.

Ten minutes into the practice, Coach Keefer had already seen and heard enough. He stopped the drills and called everyone together. He went down a laundry list of all the things that had gone wrong: the tardiness, the cornrows, the attitude. "You guys aren't ready to practice," he said. "Go to the locker room, don't shower, and get out of here as quickly as you can. If you come back tomorrow with the same attitude, I'll kick you out again." It was yet another wake-up call for a team that had a lot of work to do if it was going to defend the legacy, as the T-shirts stated.

Nobody was late for the next practice. Anthony Oden's cornrows were gone. The team's mouths were zipped shut. Coach Keefer finally had his team's full attention. Practice began with an initial tension in the air, which quickly transformed into an intensity level that was almost unbearable. During a three-on-two drill, one of the guards missed a shot that softly bounced off the back of the rim. As one player lazily jumped for a defensive rebound, Warren Wallace leaped over him and slammed the rebound through the hoop with a spectacular one-handed dunk. It had become that kind of practice.

The coaches huddled together well after the third practice had ended, deciding who to cut from the squad. Early conversation centered around two sophomores: Marcus Isaac and Cameron Carlton. Issac, a wiry guard who could put points on the board in a hurry, was cut as a freshman even though he was a local legend at the Fall Creek YMCA. Put him in a playground setting, where defense is not at a premium, and he could just light up the older guys he played against. Carlton was a transfer from Brebeuf Jesuit and a tremendous athlete capable of throwing down a 360-degree dunk. But despite his leaping ability, he was not a skilled basketball player. Working against Carlton was the fact that he had moved into the Lawrence North district in November, only days before the start of practice. The coaches knew he could jump out of the gym, but hadn't had enough time to evaluate his overall talent.

The debate among the coaches became intense. "When I go see other teams play, they always have athletes like Carlton," Coach Keefer argued. "None of our guys can do that. As far as skills, well, he hasn't been with us the past two years. You guys can teach him those things." They ultimately decided to keep both players.

The kid the coaches decided to cut was Tony Bent, a 6-foot-2, 265-pound junior who had received a championship ring last season. Bent was a very good inside player, with solid post moves. But in an up-and-down game, he just wasn't fast enough to fit into the team's plans. Keefer had a 6-foot-8 forward, Jeremy Henderson, who had played with Oden, Conley, and Brandon McDonald on the Craig Middle School team, then moved out of state. Now he was back, and his presence could fill some of the interior void left by the subtraction of Bent. Keefer also had Greg Oden's younger brother, Anthony, to help out inside.

Keefer could justify cutting Bent in the long run as well. For next year, he had two tall eighth graders waiting in the wings. It was difficult to justify a roster spot for a 6-foot-2 center on a team with that much height—not even counting Oden. Still, Keefer was torn. "How do you cut a kid you gave a ring to six months ago?" he asked. Bent had never gotten close to the coach, and that ultimately informed Keefer's decision. "You know, if you are trying to make a team, you may want to be nice to the head coach," he said. "Tony is just not nice to me."

Sometimes basketball decisions can be that easy.

Three days before the first game of the season, Oden showed up at a team dinner in obvious discomfort thanks to a swollen knee. On first evaluation the team doctor predicted that Oden could have a tear of the meniscus cartilage, which would require arthroscopic surgery. If that scenario proved true, the Wildcats would be without their star for several weeks. A magnetic resonance imaging (MRI) would render the verdict.

Coach Etherington was the high-strung guy on the staff, and the possibility of having to start the season without Oden was enough to send him into a fit of worry. But the fit was short; the MRI turned up negative—there was no major structural damage to Oden's knee. Doctors declared it a nasty bruise and cleared him to play in the opener against Lawrence Central. With the doc's blessing, Oden got down to business. Before a sold-out Lawrence North crowd, he dominated the game with 26 points, going 11 of 12 from the field, including several jump shots. After the game, which the Wildcats won 77-43, Keefer told reporters that Oden would be counted on for his offense from now on.

"His freshman year, he played a lot of defense and scored with a rebound or two," Keefer said. "As a sophomore, his offense improved. But now he can be a major force with his offense. We're working on getting the ball to him more, and I love his decision making. If he's open, he'll make a move. If not, he kicks it back out. He has come leaps and bounds from where he used to be."

The Wildcats handily dominated Brebeuf Jesuit in the second game of the season, winning 71-37. Oden's influence was felt on two vastly different plays. First, as a trailer on a fast break, Oden snagged the rebound on a teammate's missed layup—which bounded high in the air—with his right hand, switched the ball to his left hand in mid-air, and dunked before his feet touched the floor. Later in the game a Brebeuf guard went up for a seemingly open three-point shot only to be startled by Oden's long arms fast approaching to block his shot. He came down with the ball still in his hands and was whistled for a traveling violation.

The locker room was not all smiles after the game, however. There was a casualty: Conley had injured his big toe when his shoe came off as he was running down the court. He had jammed his toe into the court, and was forming a deep bruise. Unlike Oden's knee, the problem would not go away so swiftly. Still, Conley would attempt to play through the pain.

There was also an incident at the end of the game with Zach Stewart, whose poor attitude had already raised Coach Keefer's ire in the first practice of the season. Stewart got into the game in the fourth quarter with Lawrence North up by 33 points. He went to the free throw line four times and missed three of the shots. His failure to convert the free throws wasn't the problem; it was the manner in which he missed them. To the coaching staff, it appeared as if Stewart was intentionally missing the free throws, as if to say he was too good to be on the court during mop-up time. When he followed the misses by running up from behind a Brebeuf Jesuit player and trying to steal the ball—a strictly playground move—Keefer called a time-out and met Stewart at half-court. "Zach, what are you doing?" he demanded. "Don't be an asshole out here." Keefer knew Stewart had an attitude. He had started his high school career at Pike, then transferred to Lawrence North with the attitude that his playing time should be a guaranteed occurrence. But in truth, he didn't fit well into the Wildcats system and probably should have transferred someplace else where he could receive more playing time. Stewart was an unhappy player, and Keefer wanted to try to nip it in the bud.

After the game, Keefer felt guilty that he'd called Stewart an asshole. "You didn't," Coach Shelt informed him. "You told him not to be an asshole."

Keefer grinned. "I guess you're right."

The third game of the year was at Terre Haute South, the high school Oden would have attended had he not moved to Indianapolis. It was the Wildcats' first close game of the year, but the team held together and pulled it out, 52-40. Stewart played sparingly in the game, and his father came down to the court after the game to express his displeasure.

With that, Coach Keefer had discovered his problem child for the season.

Greg Oden at the 2003 Nike All-American Basketball Camp in Indianapolis. Dilip Vishwanat/TSN/Icon SMI

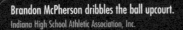

Brandon McPherson dribbles the ball upcourt.
Indiana High School Athletic Association, Inc.

Stefan Routt releases a shot in the lane.
Indiana High School Athletic Association, Inc.

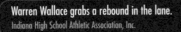

Warren Wallace grabs a rebound in the lane.
Indiana High School Athletic Association, Inc.

Lawrence North assistant coach Jim Emerington. Photo by David Dixon

Former Lawrence North assistant coach J.R. Shelt, with Greg Oden. Indiana High School Athletic Association, Inc.

Lawrence North assistant coach Ralph Scott. Photo by David Dixon

Greg Oden backs his defender down and prepares to score. Indiana High School Athletic Association, Inc.

Mike Conley and Greg Oden announce their intent to play college ball at Ohio State University at a press conference at Lawrence North on June 29, 2005.
AJ Mast/Icon SMI

The Wildcats celebrate their 2005 Indiana state championship.
Indiana High School Athletic Association, Inc.

Mike Conley drives around his defender.
Photo by David Dixon

Brandon McDonald attempts an open jump shot.
Photo by David Dixon

Qadr Owen penetrates for a lay-up.
Photo by David Dixon

Damian Windham makes his move to the basket. Photo by David Dixon

Greg Oden and Mike Conley were named McDonald's All-Americans during their senior season. Photo by David Dixon

Months earlier, Lawrence North had been contacted by Paragon Marketing Group, a Skokie, Illinois, company that brokered high school games to ESPN. In 2002, Paragon was responsible for pitching a dream game to ESPN2: LeBron James and his St. Vincent-St. Mary high school team against the No. 1 team in the country, Oak Hill Academy in Virginia. The sports network jumped on the idea, and the December game was broadcast with Dick Vitale and Bill Walton as announcers. The game was seen in 1.67 million homes and gained a 1.97 rating, ESPN2's highest in two years.

Since that landmark game, Paragon had produced six high school games for ESPN, always involving high-profile players such as James or future NBA lottery draft pick Dwight Howard. They called Coach Keefer to propose a game between Lawrence North and Poplar Bluff, the defending Missouri state champion which featured Tyler Hansbrough, a 6-foot-9 forward who would go on to average 18.9 points a game in his freshman season at North Carolina the following year.

ESPN had never before broadcast a game with a high school junior as the featured attraction, but agreed that Oden would generate hype. Paragon told Keefer that Lawrence North would receive $5,000 for the rights to broadcast, and they would pay for Poplar Bluff's trip to Indianapolis to play at Hinkle Fieldhouse. And they reminded Keefer that the matchup would put a national spotlight on Lawrence North and its basketball program.

They weren't kidding. Never in their lives had any of the Lawrence North coaching staff imagined playing a high school basketball game on national television. The week of the game, *Sports Illustrated* published a six-page profile of Oden that all but proclaimed him as the top pick of the 2006 draft. Oden reacted to the publicity in typical fashion, shrugging it off. But his teammates were excited, knowing that college coaches across the country would be tuned in to the game. This was their chance to impress.

Before the Poplar Bluff game, rumors began to circulate through the media that the Wildcat coaches wouldn't discipline Oden or Conley out of a fear that the duo would transfer to a prep school. Every time someone mentioned it, the coaches rolled their eyes. Suspend them for what? They were model students and team players. The coaches were pretty sure they knew where the rumor originated—a parent who wasn't happy with simply watching his kid's team win. This parent wanted his son on the court and wanted to watch him score.

The rumors may have served as a subtle distraction for some reporters, but the majority of the media coverage focused on the matchup of big men: Hansbrough versus Oden. One such article appeared in *The Indianapolis Star*, and Coach Keefer latched onto it as a motivational tool. He posted the article in the locker room, and reminded his players that they won and they lost as a team. "If that's all they're going to print, then the hell with them," Keefer told the team. "Greg knows this team would win without him, and we know Greg would win with four other players. We are a team. It's not Greg Oden versus Tyler what's-his-name? Do you understand? It's *we*; it's *us* against them. We must all do our jobs and we will win together. But if you don't do your part, then we'll get beat."

With the cameras rolling, Lawrence North came out tight—particularly Oden, who admitted to being flustered by the bright lights of ESPN. He took just two shots in the first half. As the Wildcats walked off the court at halftime down 26-23, the television announcers seemed a little embarrassed that a player they had relentlessly hyped was tanking in front of their eyes.

At the break, Shelt pulled Oden aside. "Greg," he said. "What are you worried about? What are you afraid of? Just go out there and play basketball." Oden thought about it for a moment, then looked Coach Shelt in the eyes and responded with an emphatic, "Yeah!" The second half buzzer sounded, and like a heavyweight champion responding to the ding of the bell, Oden took over the game. During one stretch of the third quarter, he scored 11 of his team's 13 points, including four dunks in a row. One of those dunks—an alley-oop from Brandon Coffer—was on *SportsCenter* later that night as a Top-10 highlight. The Wildcats pulled away with ease, winning 56-40. Oden finished with a team-high 16 points, and Donald Cloutier played the best game of his life, scoring 15 in keeping the game close during the first half.

By the end of the game, Oden had made believers out of the once-hesitant Vitale and Walton. ESPN analyst Jay Bilas said flatly, "I think he may be the best center prospect in the country … maybe even in the world." Hansbrough might have agreed, having encountered a new problem during the game: the need to alter his shot. Used to simply shooting over his opponents, the future college star noted after the game, "I had to shot-fake a lot and try to avoid his long arms."

More than 7,000 fans saw the game in person, including a large contingent of NBA scouts, and a respectable 629,000 viewers tuned in to the game on television. The Wildcats had gone into the game ranked seventh in the nation by *USA Today*, and with their convincing win, were likely to climb even higher. The game had served another purpose: boosting Lawrence North's chances of winning the unofficial national championship. Beating a top team from out of state was a huge step in that direction. The Wildcats had the best player in the country. They were undefeated. They had just won on ESPN. The team and its fans were riding high.

Which is why nobody should have been surprised by what happened next.

The Wildcats traveled to Fort Wayne Snider two days after the ESPN game to play in front of 4,500 people at Memorial Coliseum. On the first play of the game, a Fort Wayne player shoved his knee into Brandon McPherson's thigh. The Lawrence North coaches thought it was a blatant cheap shot, and it hobbled McPherson for the rest of the game. Snider hung close early in the game thanks to hot outside shooting, and trailed the Wildcats by only three points at the half. When Oden went to the bench with three fouls early in the third quarter, Snider went on a tear to outscore Lawrence North 21-10. No one had ever manhandled the Wildcats like that during the Oden-Conley era, and a confident Fort Wayne team took a 10-point lead into the fourth quarter. The Wildcats responded with a run of their own, and outscored Snider 28-10 to eke out a 10-point win. Conley paced the Wildcats on a bum toe with 21 points, 11 rebounds, and nine assists. But there was plenty to work on at the next practice: Lawrence North converted just 36.7 percent of their free throws, and Oden went just 3 of 12 from the line.

They had a full week to steady themselves for a road game against conference rival Indianapolis Arlington. But their attitude leading up to the key early-season matchup did not impress Coach Keefer. There were eight seniors on the Lawrence North team, and six of them showed up late for the trip to Arlington. Keefer was livid. A little swagger was good for a 6-0 team, but this was over-board. This was taking things for granted. In the locker room before the game, Keefer reamed out his team. "You're going to go out there to play Arlington and get your asses kicked," he warned. And that's exactly what happened.

Going into the game, the Wildcats were nursing two major injuries. McPherson was still limping from the incident in Fort Wayne. He didn't practice the entire week and still couldn't move well. Of greater concern was Conley. He reinjured his toe against Snider and could barely walk before the Arlington game. Conley tried to play, but couldn't push off. He ended up watching most of the game from the bench. Oden tried to make up the difference, scoring 25 points, but didn't touch the ball down the stretch. Without Conley, the Wildcats were unsuccessful at adjusting to the Arlington defense, and couldn't feed it down to him. Lawrence North battled back to within two points with just under two minutes left, but Arlington held on to beat them, 70-60.

Any dreams of an undefeated season were over, but Lawrence North had worse problems to contend with. They knew they could win without Oden; but what were they going to do without Conley?

Donald Cloutier dunks the ball. Indiana High School Athletic Association, Inc.

EIGHT

The prognosis was not good for Conley. He was diagnosed with "turf toe," a debilitating injury to the joint linking the toe to the foot, which would keep him out as long as four weeks. The only good news was the timing: Lawrence North was in the soft part of its schedule because of the Christmas holidays, and had just three games before the county tournament started January 10. The coaching staff held out the hope that Conley could return by then.

Conley, like Oden, is an incredibly humble young man. Yet on the court, he has a coolness about him and plays the game so effortlessly that he has been accused of just going through the motions. He does not show a lot of emotion—on or off the court. But Conley chalks it up to his personality. "I don't get too high," he says. "I'm working but just don't show agony." His presence has a positive impact on his teammates, who look to their point guard at times of need and find a calm, collected soul.

With a ball in hand, Conley is an explosive player. He can dribble—and shoot—with either hand. A natural right-hander in most activities, he began shooting left-handed when he was just five years old and continues to do so today. "I didn't know you should have a certain hand," he says. His ambidexterity had helped him overcome an injury to his left thumb during a summer tournament. After sitting out one game, he became antsy and decided to shoot right-handed in the next contest so that he could play. He ended up delivering his team to a come-from-behind victory with a string of threes—all of which came on shot attempts with his off hand.

What makes Conley such a complete player is that despite his offensive talent, he doesn't neglect his duties on defense. Often drawing the defensive assignment of guarding the opponent's top backcourt scorer, Conley is able to shut down even the most talented shooters due to his supreme quickness, tenacity, and confidence derived from having faced older players throughout much of his life. "I became used to certain moves and could anticipate them," he explains. "I take a lot of pride in my defense. If they score, I take it personal."

With Conley on the mend, it was up to the balance of the Wildcat roster to take things personally.

For their first game minus Conley, the Wildcats squared off against their second out-of-state foe of the season, undefeated Detroit Romulus High School, in the Circle City Classic

Challenge of Champions at Hinkle Fieldhouse. Zach Stewart replaced Conley in the starting line-up, and the game began as a see-saw battle. Oden faced a tough, physical double-team. Detroit Romulus tried everything—even bear hugs—to try to contain Oden. But Lawrence North was simply too talented for the northerners to handle. With the score knotted at 20-20, the Wildcats launched a 17-3 streak to break the game open.

Oden had the highlight of the night when he grabbed a defensive rebound, dribbled the length of the floor, executed a cross-over dribble to fake out a defender, and finally scored with a finger roll lay up that brought the crowd at Hinkle to its feet. With Conley— who had himself started enough fast breaks to fill a highlight reel—on the bench, Oden did it all himself. "I was going to pass," Oden said after the game. "[The defender] stepped in my way, so that's why I went back to my right. When I shot it, I thought [a foul would be called]. I just tried to throw it up to get a blocking foul, but it went in."

With Oden leading the way—scoring 22 points with 11 rebounds, three steals, and two assists—Lawrence North beat Detroit Romulus, 86-66. Everyone stepped up in Conley's absence: Brandon McPherson scored 19 points, Zach Stewart added 14, and Warren Wallace chipped in 11. It was a resounding turnaround from the team's first loss of the season.

But a legitimate scare was right around the corner. The following week Lawrence North hosted the once-beaten Franklin Central Flashes, and found itself in a real dogfight. Junior Wildcat guard Tyler Morris had broken his nose in the Detroit game and was staring down the possibility of surgery. Just like that, the depth at guard that the Wildcats once had was all but gone. And it put the hurt on the Wildcats against the Flashes.

Lawrence North played catch-up all night. Oden was triple-teamed throughout the game, and the Flashes were sharp from the floor, nailing 63 percent of their field goals in the first half. In the third quarter, the Wildcats were down by eight points, and Oden was being swallowed by the triple-team. Someone had to step up, and that someone was Stewart. The volatile guard caught fire from the outside, which finally opened up the lane for Oden. Lawrence North pulled ahead in the fourth quarter to eke out a 54-49 victory.

Following the game, Oden sat on the bench, exhausted. A long line of kids surrounded him, hounding him for his autograph. After his initial hesitation as a freshman, signing his name over and over again had become second nature, and he was always generous with his time. Celebrity had singled out Oden, and he was finally accepting the terms.

Earlier in the season, the Wildcats had headed to Bloomington to watch the North Carolina Tarheels work out prior to a game against Indiana. The team stopped at a restaurant to eat, and a man approached Oden for an autograph. Oden tried to oblige, but the man's pen wouldn't write. One of Oden's teammates offered his pen, but Oden said, "It's okay, I've got one," producing a Sharpie from his pocket. Coach Scott watched the scene unfold and teased Oden after the man walked away. "A Sharpie?" he asked. "Who do you think you are, T.O. or somebody?", referring to an end zone stunt pulled by NFL wide receiver Terrell Owens.

It would take quite a successful stunt if the Wildcats were going to win the annual Marion County Tournament without Conley, who still hadn't recovered from his injury. A highly antic-ipated matchup between Lawrence North and North Central loomed ahead. Eric Gordon, who had played with Oden and Conley on the Spiece Indy Heat AAU team that summer, had blossomed into a huge scoring threat for North Central, and Coach Keefer worried about him. "We're facing quite a chore," Keefer told *The Indianapolis Star.* "[Gordon] can score from about anywhere." Gordon was just a sophomore, but he was already drawing rave reviews from opponents and recruiting experts alike. Within a year, he would become one of the most highly regarded guards in the nation. But on January 10, 2005, he was already on the Wildcats' radar.

Lawrence North opened the game with a set play for Stewart to come off a double pick for a three-pointer. When he missed the shot, it seemed to set the tone of the game. Gordon hit his first shot, a three-pointer, and North Central broke out to a devastating 17-3 lead. The Panthers shut down Oden by applying a variation of the "hack a Shaq" technique utilized from time to time by NBA teams hoping to neutralize Shaquille O'Neal. By fouling Oden in a fashion that did not allow him an easy attempt on a field goal, they sent him to the line for two free throws instead of allowing an easy basket. The strategy worked; Oden went to the line nine times and hit only three free throws. He didn't make a shot from the floor the entire first half.

The Wildcats regrouped at the half, and McPherson led a second-half charge that enabled the Wildcats to pull to within two points with 17 seconds left. From that point, no North Central player touched the ball other than Eric Gordon. The game rested in his hands, or more specifically on his ability to convert free throws. He hit six straight shots from the charity stripe to hand Lawrence North its second defeat of the season, 69-63, and bounce them from the tournament.

Oden finished the game with just 10 points and took only five shots from the floor. To Coach Keefer, that was inexcusable. Even if three people were guarding him, they were all going to be much shorter than Oden. All he had to do was turn around and shoot it, a concept lost on Oden on this night. So Keefer instituted a new edict: The 15-shot Rule. "Greg," he said, "if you don't shoot at least 15 times in a game, then you don't start the game after that." The message was clear: Oden was to shoot the damn ball, and often. If Lawrence North was to fare any better in its rematch with North Central just 11 days later, then Oden had to accept this rule as golden.

Even with North Central's Gordon on the bench because of a bruised knee, Lawrence North started the rematch on a sloppy note. Coach Keefer called a time-out just 75 seconds into the game and lit into his team. The tongue-lashing sparked the Wildcats, as over the next 86 seconds they scored eight points. Donald Cloutier scored off an offensive rebound, and Oden showed off his complete arsenal with a dunk, a short jumper, and a lay-up. Now it was North Central's turn to take a time-out.

Playing on their home court, Lawrence North built an insurmountable lead, easily dispensing of the Panthers by a 29-point margin. Oden finished the game with 37 points on 16-of-22 shooting. Message received, loud and clear. "We're trying to gain our respect back," Oden said after the game. They were well on their way.

Coach Keefer had laid down the law—the offense went through Greg Oden. When Stewart launched a three-pointer against North Central and missed, he heard about it from Keefer. It was Stewart's moment to step up and seize the playing time he so valued. But he wasn't buying into the game plan, and the coaching staff was losing interest in him, while counting the days until Conley could return to the court.

Keefer took action: Tyler Morris was now a starter; Stewart was headed back to the bench. Morris was able to play despite his nose injury, and his toughness was evident on the court. After so many practices spent guarding Conley, he was polished on defense. More importantly, he did exactly what the coaches asked him to do. Lawrence North easily dispensed of Warren Central, then Indianapolis Broad Ripple and Center Grove. While the team flourished, Stewart's father fumed. The elder Stewart complained to Coach Shelt that he wasn't happy that his son was now back on the bench. He took the argument further, claiming that the decision was based on race since Morris was white and his son was from a mixed racial background. Shelt dismissed the racist charge as a lack of class. After all, Stewart had been given first dibs on the starting role. In the coaches' eyes, he simply failed.

The argument was a moot point when Conley finally returned after missing six games—two of which the Wildcats lost—for an important showdown with Carmel at Lawrence North's gym. The packed house included college and NBA scouts who wanted to see the matchup between Oden, the top junior in the country, and Carmel's 6-foot-10 senior, Josh McRoberts, who had committed to Duke and was considered by many experts to be the top senior in the nation. McRoberts and Oden knew each other well, having played together on the Spiece Indy Heat team. The media keyed in on the battle of big men, but Coach Keefer once again refused to allow his team to think of the game in terms of individuals. Nor did he allow his big man to tackle McRoberts on defense. Instead, he double-teamed McRoberts with Cloutier, who was 6-foot-7 and muscular, and Warren Wallace, who was just 6-foot-3 but guarded Oden every day in practice. Oden was their security blanket. Anytime McRoberts would get past one of them, Oden would have their back.

The strategy worked: McRoberts was held to just 12 points, and that included a desperation, half-court shot he hit at the buzzer. Oden, meanwhile, finished with 20 points and 12 rebounds as Lawrence North won 53-49. The Kodak moment came when a tipped Wildcat pass that appeared headed over the top of the backboard was snared in mid-flight by Oden and emphatically slammed for two points.

"He's the best player in the country," McRoberts said after the game. "We did what we could to slow him down, but you're not going to completely shut him down."

It was Oden's second media-hyped matchup against a prominent big man, and his second K.O.

Only four games remained in the Wildcats' regular season. They took care of Ben Davis High to improve their record to 14-2, with a couple significant games on the horizon against Pike and Bloomington South. With their loss at Bloomington South last season on their minds, Lawrence North was ready for sweet revenge when the 17-2 Panthers paid a visit to the Wildcats' home turf. Bloomington South, hungry for another upset, hit their first five shots of the game to jump out to a 14-4 lead. The hot start was but one of the Wildcats' worries. Before the buzzer could even draw the first quarter to a close, Oden was on the bench with three fouls.

The stakes were high, especially with Oden on the bench for the balance of the first half. That summer, Lawrence North had participated in the Indiana University team camp; Oden sprained his ankle and didn't play in an exhibition game against Arlington that the Wildcats won in overtime. In the huddle, the coaches reminded the team of that scrimmage, and told them to have confidence that they could again win without the big fellow.

Conley and McPherson responded, and the aggressive Wildcats outscored the Panthers 18-11 in the second quarter to go up 32-27. At the start of the third quarter, Oden returned to action with purpose. He scored eight of Lawrence North's first nine points of the half. On one play, Oden stole a pass and tapped the ball to McPherson, then on the other end of the court threw down an ally-oop pass for a tomahawk dunk. Conley and Oden each scored 16 points, and McPherson added 13 as Lawrence North pulled away for a 20-point win, 71-51.

Three days later, the Wildcats traveled to Pike for one of the most anticipated games of the year. Pike was 20-1, winners of the Marion County Tournament and ranked No. 2 in the state; Lawrence North, now 15-2, was ranked No. 4. Pike was the one team each season the Lawrence North players wanted to beat, and the coaches made sure this year held extra incentive. The last time the Wildcats had traveled to Pike, McPherson was a sophomore and had sent the game into overtime with two clutch free throws, before the Wildcats lost steam, and the game. Now was the time for payback. It was time to send a message that Lawrence North was still the team to beat in the state tournament that year.

Pike had a major matchup problem: its center was just 6-foot-3, which meant his head barely reached Oden's shoulders. Pike Coach Larry Bullington professed that he wasn't sure how they were going to defend Oden. "You have to try to impede his progress," he told reporters before the game. "You just can't let him run down the floor and get where he wants to on the block. We have to try to keep a body on him, and have a couple of guys around him as best we can."

But the Lawrence North coaches snickered at Bullington's comments; they knew he always conceded to Oden, letting him have his points while trying to shut down his supporting cast. And that mind-set had served him well; although Oden had always scored big against Pike, his heroics had not always brought victories for Lawrence North.

In the pregame talk, Coach Keefer emphasized the need to get off to a quick start. He wanted to build a lead and then bury Pike in the second half. As expected, Oden was getting his: he had 10 points in the first quarter alone. But his teammates were stepping up as well. McDonald started the game with a dunk, and the Wildcats defense was suffocating Pike to the tune of just four points in the first quarter. Oden picked up where he left off in the second quarter, eventually finishing the game with 28 points, 17 rebounds, and four blocked shots. But more importantly, Lawrence North had made a very big statement, beating the No. 2 team in the state 59-40.

Lawrence North's final game of the regular season was a road trip to Terre Haute North. Stewart had suffered a concussion in the game against Bloomington South, which caused him to miss the Pike game as well. The team trainer also told him he had to sit out the Terre Haute game, because under state rules a player has to sit out a certain number of games after such a head injury. Before the game, Stewart's parents confronted the trainer about the enforcement of such a policy. Coach Shelt rushed over to intervene. Defending the innocent trainer, who was only doing her job and following orders, Shelt quickly got to the point: "She had nothing to do with it," Shelt said. "You call yourselves God-fear-ing people. To yell at someone who has nothing to do with it, it's just not right. If you're mad at us, you're mad at us. Yell at us all you want. But you're not going to yell at our trainer." The parents apologized, but it was not a pleasant way to begin the final regular-season game of the year.

Still, the Wildcats retained focus and won easily, 75-44. Since losing to North Central in the Marion County Tournament, the Wildcats had rolled off nine straight victories. To win state, however, it would take another seven.

Lawrence North had five days to prepare for the first game of the state sectionals. Lurking ahead in the second game of the brackets was a possible rematch with the Arlington Golden Knights, who had given the Wildcats their first loss of the season. Arlington had yet to lose themselves; at 23-0, they were the top-ranked team in the state and the No. 3-ranked team in the country.

Lawrence North entered the state tournament in good health. Conley was again playing at 100 percent, and the team was injury-free. Oden, meanwhile, had morphed into the dominating sensation everyone expected him to become as a junior. Coach Keefer's prescription of 15 shots per night had Oden's offensive game on the upswing. A once-timid player on offense, Oden now had a tenacity to his game that was helping his team dominate their opponents.

Oden finished the 2004-05 regular season averaging 21 points, 10.1 rebounds, and 3.3 blocks per contest. Coach Keefer was proud of his latest Goliath, and as usual was diverting the praise away from himself. "[Eric] Montross, his junior year, he just came on like gangbusters," Keefer told *The Indianapolis Star.* "The same thing happened with John Stewart. You just don't make a big kid overnight. They're tall, but having the skills to go with being tall is something else. Coach Scott has done a great job" developing Oden.

Lawrence North quickly disposed of Indianapolis Manual in the first game of the sectionals, 65-27. That set up the game with Arlington, a battle between the No. 1 and No. 3 teams in the state. In the minds of many, this was the real state championship matchup—in just the second game of the sectionals. Arlington had a built-in advantage: the security that came with their defeat of Lawrence North earlier that season. "Even though we beat them, about 95 percent of the people still think we're underdogs," claimed Arlington senior Deonta Vaughn, who had scorched Lawrence North for 31 points in their initial matchup. "But we'll come out to try to prove our point."

The game was played in the Lawrence Central gym, which seats just 3,000 people. Considering the magnitude of the game, it should have been moved to the more spacious Hinkle Fieldhouse. When it was announced that the remaining 600 tickets would go on sale the day of the game at 5 p.m., a line started forming at 2 p.m. even though it was a cold and blustery afternoon. By game time, 600 people were lined up at the front door—plus another 600 at the rear door—hoping to get tickets. Hundreds of fans were turned away.

Among those who were lucky enough to crowd into the gym were Ohio State head coach Thad Matta, Wake Forest head coach Skip Prosser, and North Carolina assistant coach Joe Holliday. All three were there to watch Conley, but all three also held out hope that Oden might forego the draft, even if for one year of college experience. What they saw that night was a Hoosier basketball classic that had just about everything you could ever hope to see in a high school game.

Coach Shelt had scouted Arlington for the Wildcats, and in the locker room before the game he delivered a potent, passionate message to the team. "They think they're tougher than you," Shelt told the boys. "They think you're suburban sweethearts." He turned to Conley. "Mike, they don't know why you get all this attention. They don't think you're that good." Then he turned to Morris. "Tyler, they want to know how you got a scholarship offer. No one's offering their kids scholarships, and here's this little 5-foot-11 white kid and you get a scholarship offer? How?" Shelt then addressed the entire team again. "They've got a chip on their shoulder, and you guys have got some things to prove to them. They're not tougher than we are. You guys go out there and show them that. Last time they won. But we're better than that now. It's going to be a fight the whole game."

And a fight it was. Arlington's game plan was to drive the lane and go directly at Oden in the hopes of coercing a foul call. With Oden on the bench in foul trouble, the Golden Knights felt they could contend with the Wildcats. The game quickly turned physical, but the referees' whistles remained silent; they were content to let each team play its game. The physical play fired up the crowd and filled the gym with an electric atmosphere. Fans rooting for both Arlington and Lawrence North were shouting at the officials in turns, for fouls both called and imagined. When the refs failed to respond to the taunts, each side's fans began screaming at one another across the court.

Early on, there was a moment where things almost turned ugly. Conley drove to the basket and was fouled hard. He fell to the floor, followed by an Arlington player who landed on top of him. The Arlington kid was slow to get up. Rather than jerk around and try to push the player off of him, which might have inspired a fight, Conley—cool and collected as usual—crossed his arms behind his head, laid his head in his hands, and just relaxed until the player got off of him. Then Conley stood up, straightened his uniform, and swished his free throws.

But that was not the end of it for Conley. A few minutes later, he shrugged off a dirty play when Arlington's Anthony Munford elbowed him to the floor during a dead ball. Conley was content to let his team's play do the talking. But on the court, the Wildcats were struggling to gain the upper hand.

Early on, Conley walked over to Oden and asked, "We gonna lose this game, Greg?"

Oden shook his head. "No way we're gonna lose this game."

And it became a saying between them for the rest of the game: "We gonna lose this game?" "Nah, no way we're gonna lose this game."

But losing, it was: At halftime, Lawrence North was down, 35-32. The coaches felt Arlington's intent was to try to beat them up in addition to just beating them, like the old Detroit Pistons "Bad Boys" teams of the late '80s. But Lawrence North refused to back down to the intimidation, which took the edge off of Arlington's players. They were used to dominating their opponents, beating down a team with their full-court press and physical play. But the Wildcats wouldn't give in. And the Golden Knights' strategy of attacking Oden wasn't working out as planned: All those drives inside by Arlington had resulted in plenty of blocked shots for Oden, including three on a single possession.

Coach Keefer focused his halftime speech on taking Arlington's crowd out of the game with a strong start to the half. Lawrence North did better than that. Executing their coach's plan to a T, the Wildcats went on a 16-0 run in the third quarter. Arlington was so shaken up by Lawrence North's resilience in the first half and the sudden charge in the second, that they forgot all about Deonta Vaughn, their star player and one of the best seniors in the state. Arlington's offensive game plan was quite simple: ride Vaughn to victory. It had worked in the two teams' first meeting that season, but now he was barely getting any shots off. Nothing was coming easy for the star guard, and the deeper the game went, the more frustrated he became. In the end, the Wildcats' will proved stronger, as Lawrence North protected their lead down the stretch for a 60-45 victory. It was Arlington's lowest point total of the season; Oden's 18 blocks had played a large role in the outcome.

After the game, Coach Keefer praised his team's toughness, calling the win a matter of survival. Coach Shelt was later asked if Lawrence North felt like the underdogs against an undefeated team that was ranked third in the nation and had already defeated the Wildcats once. "Never," he said. "We are state champs, not them. Everybody said all season, this was the game. The winner would go on to win state. And both sides believed it. But ... until somebody beats us, we're the champs. So we never had the feeling that we were the underdog. We expected to win. We knew going in we were going to get it. There was no doubt."

A headline in *The Indianapolis Star* summed up the game perfectly: "Hoosier hysteria, like in the old days."

It seemed almost an afterthought when Lawrence North won the sectionals the next evening, beating Indianapolis Cathedral 39-30. Cathedral slowed the tempo of the game down to a crawl. After such a bruising, emotional, and fast-paced game against Arlington, Lawrence North was exhausted. Cathedral came out with a sharpness and intensity; Lawrence North played like it was running through mud. The Wildcats won, but they won with as little effort as they could afford. After the game, the coaches were not happy. If they played like that again, it would be their last game of the season. That was a dangerous proposition at that moment, because next up for the Wildcats was a showdown with the 22-3 Pike Red Devils at Hinkle.

The day of regionals is the most brutal single day in high school basketball: To emerge from the bracket victorious, a team has to win two games in one day against the best teams in the state. More than 6,500 fans crammed inside Hinkle for the 10 a.m. tip off. Thanks to a week off between games, the Wildcats came out energized—maybe too energized. Oden was called for the first technical foul of his career for hanging on the rim. He went up for a dunk and lost control of the ball. He grabbed hold of the rim to catch his balance and was hit with a T.

The Wildcats pulled ahead early, going up by two points at the end of the first quarter before building their lead to 26-19 at the half. By the end of the third, their lead was eight, but Pike refused to go quietly. The Red Devils hit a three-pointer and then a foul shot to pull to within four points with a little over three minutes left to play. The Wildcats pounded the ball inside to Oden, who was swarmed as he made a move to the basket. He was able to get his shot off, and the ball rolled around the rim in dramatic fashion before finally going in. Two points plus the foul. Oden hit the free throw to put Lawrence North up by seven, and the Wildcats hung on to win 54-46.

The Saturday nightcap against North Central turned out to be Lawrence North's most interesting game of the season. Oden was still carrying a grudge from the first time the two teams had tangled that season, when North Central won by six points with Conley injured and on the bench. North Central coach Doug Mitchell had been somewhat dismissive of Oden's size advantage, talking to the press about how strong his team was thanks to North Central's advanced weight-training program. Oden thought the comments made him out to be a wimp, and he was determined to set things straight with North Central.

Oden possessed a ferocity never before revealed, and his coaches were a bit stunned. The Panthers used a stocky football player to guard Oden, and whenever the Wildcats passed it to him, Oden was deliberate and quick. He intended to punish his defender every time he touched the ball. He'd dunk, then talk trash to the kid trying in vain to defend him. This was a new development for Oden, who had never before been a trash talker. He was usually as stoic on the court as Robert Parish, the Big Chief of the Boston Celtics. But his aggression in this game was astounding, so much so that he was showing up his opponents, clapping his hands and glaring at the Panthers after scoring. His adrenaline flowing, he lost focus on defense and got himself into foul trouble. Conley soon followed suit. Both were called for their third foul early in the first half and had to sit on the bench for an extended period of time.

Lawrence North knew it could win without Oden, and it knew it could win without Conley. That much had been proven. But it had been three years since they'd had to find a way to win without Oden *and* Conley. To compensate for the loss of their two star players, Lawrence North turned to the basics: defense. From the 2:45 mark in the first quarter, when North Central hit a three, until there was 3:30 left in the third, the Panthers didn't make a single basket. The Wildcats held North Central to 0-17 shooting over that time frame. Still, at halftime, Lawrence North was up by just four points, 35-31, largely thanks to Tyler Morris' hot hand filling in for Conley.

Oden re-entered the game to score nine points in the third quarter. But both he and Conley had to return to the bench after each picked up their fourth foul. Again Morris came off the bench to carry the team, and Lawrence North eventually pulled away to a 56-42 victory. Oden tallied 17 points in 24 minutes of play, and Morris added 12 points in Conley's absence.

After the game, Oden told the press he was trying to play with emotion. "Coach [Keefer] has always told me that when I'm hungry, that's when I'm playing," Oden said. "So I decided to talk, because I really wanted to win this game."

The coaches did want emotion, but trash-talking was not a part of that equation, and they talked to him about his behavior afterwards. Mike Conley Sr. also pulled him aside to make a point. "Who do you want to be like?" he asked Oden. "You've always said you wanted to be like Shaq. That's not something Shaq would have done. Shaq's not that kind of player. And you're not that kind of player. You don't want to be *seen* as that kind of player."

Oden nodded his head and thanked Mr. Conley. Now he felt embarrassed. But he would allow himself no opportunity for such embarrassment again. From that point forward, he vowed to never show up another high school opponent. It was back to being the same old Greg Oden.

All season, teams had made extreme adjustments when they stepped on the court to play against Lawrence North and, more specifically, Oden. They double-teamed him and triple-teamed him. They fouled him as soon as he tried to make an offensive move, to prevent him from getting a shot off. Terre Haute South's head coach, Mike Saylor, might have come up with the most unique strategy of all: Practicing to play Lawrence North in the state semi-finals, Saylor stationed 6-foot-4 Tyler Richey in the paint with a tennis racquet. "Greg is probably the greatest shot blocker in Indiana history," Saylor explained to *The Indianapolis Star*. "You have to be smart. You have to take shots *around* him."

Of course, few strategies to combat Oden actually worked. Swatting shots with a tennis racquet was amusing, but it really didn't prepare a team to play someone as gifted and as tall as Oden. Kids on a high school level just couldn't compete with him. He was just too athletic, certainly more so than a kid with a tennis racquet.

At halftime of their semifinal matchup with Terre Haute South, the Wildcats were in complete control, up 34-19. Even more telling was that one player, Armon Bassett, had scored all of the Braves' 19 points. Coach Keefer reminded his team during the break to stick to their game plan. "I've told this to you before and I'll tell it to you again: One player cannot beat a team. Don't even worry about it."

But Morris was plenty worried about it. Bassett was his man, and he couldn't stop him. Coach Keefer pulled Morris aside. "Tyler, you're doing your job," he said. "You're making him work. He's driving, he's shooting every time, and nobody else is touching the ball. You think the other kids on the team are happy about that?"

In the second half, Bassett scored 10 more points, many of them on slashing drives to the basket, and the Braves pulled to within eight points at 52-44, with 6:18 to play. The Wildcats switched to a 1-3-1 zone to disrupt the drives to the lane. The Braves didn't have an answer for the adjustment, which allowed the Wildcats to distance themselves with a 14-0 run before eventually winning 71-52. Oden paced a balanced Wildcats attack with 20 points, while Conley added 17, McPherson scored 15, and Cloutier chipped in 11. Every time the Braves closed one option, Lawrence North went to another. "I felt like we had a rally going and a chance," a hapless Saylor said after the game. "But what do they have, four Division I players and one NBA player?"

Saylor made a good point.

The Wildcats faced one last formidable obstacle in its path for a second consecutive state championship. Maybe the win against Arlington in the sectionals was the real championship game. But the Muncie Central Bearcats were insulted by that talk. The Bearcats owned more state championship trophies—eight—than any other high school in Indiana, and also happened to be ranked No. 2 in the state with a 27-1 record. "Everyone in [our] gym knows the history of Muncie Central basketball, and they feel it's important to uphold the legacy," Muncie coach Matt Fine said before the game.

But the Wildcats had their own legacy to defend. Coach Keefer had asked them at the start of the season: What do you want your legacy to be? Their goal was at hand; it was theirs for the taking.

The Lawrence North coaches huddled to come up with their game plan. Muncie Central had three guards who could score:

Alex Daniel (13.2 points per game) played the point; Josiah Miller (13.2 points) was a slasher; and Ty Riddle (12.8 points) was an outside gun. It was Riddle who especially worried Lawrence North. He played with confidence and could stroke it from anywhere on the court.

A sell-out crowd of 18,345 people packed into Conseco Fieldhouse in downtown Indianapolis on March 26, 2005. The question on everyone's mind was simple: could Muncie Central stop Greg Oden? The answer was also simple: No. The Bearcats' 6-foot-6 defender was no match for Oden. And Conley was successful at containing Riddle. By game's end, Oden had scored 29 points on 14-of-19 shooting, and added nine rebounds and six blocked shots. McPherson, playing his final game for Lawrence North, added 11 points as the only other Wildcat to reach double figures. Lawrence North's steady assault produced a 63-52 victory.

As the 24-2 Wildcats celebrated their second straight state championship, Bearcats coach Matt Fine had little for the press but a shrug of his shoulders. "With their guys we had to play almost a perfect game, and we didn't do that," he said after the game. "And with Greg, what can you do against him?"

Before the final horn even sounded the conjecture had started: Could Lawrence North—who finished the year ranked No. 6 in the nation according to *USA Today*—do it all over again with Conley and Oden as seniors? "We've got a long time to think about that," Oden said. "When open gyms start, we'll see how we look and we'll try to get it together. We'll work hard for next year."

The difficult task was going to be rebuilding team chemistry. Oden and Conley would be playing with a young supporting cast: the Wildcats were losing several seniors, including Cloutier, Morris, and McPherson. But Keefer wasn't fretting. "Our [junior varsity] had maybe two losses. Our freshman team had some [quality players]. We've got an undefeated eighth-grade team coming in," he told *The Indianapolis Star*. "We've got a good group of kids, and we'll see what we can do with them, but I like what I've got to build on."

With Oden and Conley as the building blocks, any coach would find the odds to his liking.

Coach Keefer in the Lawrence North gym. Photo by David Dixon

NINE

Jack Keefer is a firm believer in building a bridge to future Lawrence North prospects. That commitment extends beyond making his junior varsity squad feel a part of his varsity group during practices. He also hosts a summer camp, referred to as the "Keefer Camp," for ballers aged kindergarten through eighth grade. Approximately 350 boys attend the camp, which focuses on fundamentals and includes scrimmages. A majority of the kids go home with ribbons and trophies, assuring that the camp boosts the morale of its attendants. His assistant coaches, as well as many of his own players, participate in the camp, which serves as an effective tool for broadening Lawrence North's reach into the community.

For Keefer, the goal of maintaining a high school basketball empire in a hotbed for hoops is a consuming process, and it has taken its toll. As history has proven true of many a ruler, Keefer has developed his fair share of critics and enemies. Thus is the nature of competition, especially when the competition is for the top prep talent in the state.

Terre Haute South head coach Mike Saylor is one of Keefer's vocal critics. "At one time [Lawrence North] had five transfers in grades 8-12 from Terre Haute South," he points out, speaking of Zach Stewart, Chaz Spicer, Greg and Anthony Oden, and female basketball player Racinda Russell. "There are bad feelings. If you had 10 pieces of furniture and five were stolen and ended up at somebody else's house—but you couldn't prove it—you still would feel bad."

Saylor's frustrations are understandable. After all, his team lost to Lawrence North in the 2005 state tournament semifinals. If Oden would have been on his side, chances are it might have been Terre Haute South in the finals. But consider this: Stewart first transferred to Pike before moving to Lawrence North; Spicer's family moved to Indianapolis due to a job transfer, and Keefer claims that former Terre Haute South coach Pat Rady actually recommended that Spicer attend Lawrence North. (And who could blame him, considering the program's storied past?)

Saylor believes that the Odens packed their bags in part because of a feud that had been simmering between Oden's Terre Haute AAU coach, Jimmy Smith, and Rady. "Greg was inundated by criticism [from Smith] about Pat Rady," Saylor charges. "I don't blame the Odens because of the propaganda. Jimmy Smith criticized Pat a lot when he had Greg."

Saylor's case lacks much in the way of evidence linking Keefer to one of high school sports' white elephants—recruiting. If Keefer has benefited from anything, it's Lady Luck. When the Conleys moved from Fayetteville, Arkansas, to Indianapolis due to Mike Conley Sr. being hired by USA Track & Field, they relocated to a rented home in the Indianapolis Pike school district. With most of their belongings in storage, they submitted a bid on a house in the Lawrence Central district. Enter Lady Luck: their bid was rejected. Later, they purchased a home in the Lawrence North district, and Mike Conley attended Craig Middle School, en route for Lawrence North.

"I'm just tickled to death he didn't get that house," Jack says with a satisfied smile. During his long tenure as the only basketball coach in the 30-year history of Lawrence North, he has benefited from a number of talented move-ins. Again, luck intervened with the most talented of all move-ins: Oden. Greg's relationship with the Conleys shaped his mother's decision to relocate her sons from Terre Haute to the Lawrence North district of Indianapolis, so that Greg and Mike could continue to play ball together at Craig.

Lawrence North's basketball dynasty quite possibly hinged on the sale of one house.

Keefer's Wildcats generally play archrival North Central two or three times a year—once in the regular season, often once in the Marion County Tournament, and occasionally in the state playoffs. From the fall of 2002 through the spring of 2006, the Wildcats handed the Panthers eight losses, two of those in the state tournament. North Central head coach Doug Mitchell has plenty of reason to be frustrated, and he isn't shy with voicing those frustrations with Keefer.

"Jack's approach to things and my approach are different," he says. "...We go about things from the grass roots [at North Central]. We like to think we built our program. Sure, we have an occasional transfer, but most of our kids come from our middle school program."

Mitchell, a fine coach in his own right, does admit, "The guy can coach his [rear] off. Once he gets them, he can coach them. And they play hard. Jack is an innovative guy. It's been kind of an intense rivalry from Day One. But it's always been a healthy rivalry. I believe everybody has the utmost respect for each other."

Mitchell has seen the impact Lawrence North's success has had on its appeal to young basketball players. "I think now people seek him out [to send their sons to Lawrence North]," he concedes.

Like Saylor, Mitchell has lost out on top talent thanks to transfers. Brad Leaf, Todd Leary, and Tom Geyer—the latter two both eventual Indiana All-Stars—attended North Central as younger players and transferred to Lawrence North. But each had legitimate reasons for the move.

Leaf, who was Lawrence North's first star, had never attended Keefer's summer camp, nor had he ever met him. He had, however, been on a Lawrence Township traveling team as a sixth grader and maintained a close friendship with the coach, Tom Wallace, whose son, Tom, was playing at Lawrence North. A tall, slender guard, Leaf says he was maybe the No. 8 player on North Central's varsity team as a junior and, admittedly, he was unhappy. The family moved in the middle of the basketball season. In his first game with his new Lawrence North team, he scored 20 points, even though he sat out the first quarter. From that point forward, he was a starter. Before his career was over, he would cut down the nets after scoring 25 points to defeat his former school in a tournament game.

Leaf, now a winning high school coach living in California, understands the skepticism that shadows Coach Keefer. But he echoes other sentiments: kids are attracted to winning programs. "I brag about his program all the time to my players," Leaf says. "He always treated everybody the same, [both] subs and stars."

Geyer left North Central as a freshman because he wanted to attend a smaller school with a stronger emphasis on academics. Geyer—who calls Coach Mitchell a "great guy"—was subject to plenty of teasing by his classmates due to a hearing aid he had to wear. "I wanted to go down a different path," he says. "My parents were pretty open to moving anywhere. We also considered Noblesville and Carmel. We ended up moving just two miles."

Leary had attended Keefer's summer camp for many years, even though he lived in the North Central school district. His grandparents were both Lawrence North fans, and together they grew up watching future Indiana All-Star Reed Crafton. The Leary family wound up building a new house in the Lawrence North district and moving toward the end of Todd's eighth grade year. Leary claims he was hardly a hot commodity at the time of his transfer. "I had a lot of friends at North Central," he says. "They gave me a hard time, but I always wanted to play for Coach Keefer."

Academics, environment, lack of playing time, familial influence, friendship—all are reasons for moving to another school that are hardly unique to the players transferring to Lawrence North. Take Penny Sargent for example. He had started as a freshman at rival Ben Davis High School, averaging around 17 points a game. By his sophomore year, he was a Wildcat. He explains it simply: "My family was looking for a house and found one in the Lawrence North district. I didn't know much about Coach Keefer, but I had played AAU ball with a couple of Lawrence North players. People crack jokes about [recruiting]. But if you had a chance to move and play basketball, you'd want to play at the best place." Sargent points out that when Lawrence North went 11-11 is his first season with the team, nobody said anything about recruiting.

Brandon McPherson, Sargent's teammate on the 2004 and '05 championship Wildcats, lived in the Indianapolis Arlington district. McPherson, an extremely athletic guard with a bubbly personality, had dominated Keefer's summer camp as a youngster. Entering high school, he wanted to play for Jack and only Jack. So his parents paid tuition for him to attend Lawrence North. It paid off handsomely: he collected two championship rings, and his 3.5 scholastic average helped earn him the coveted 2005 Trester Award for academics and mental attitude.

Then, there's the John Stewart story. The bulky 7-footer, who was at Lawrence Central as a freshman, languished on the junior varsity bench at Carmel High as a sophomore. He transferred yet again as a junior to Lawrence North, where the struggle began anew.

"He was unhappy where he was," Keefer recalls. "We have a reputation of treating big men well. We treat them like gold. ... [But] Stewart was overweight. The first day of practice, he walked down the floor, and I kicked him out."

Keefer found him crying in the locker room. Stewart told him, "You're not going to help me. You're just like all the other coaches."

"I *am* helping you," Jack quickly replied. "Come back tomorrow and run the stairs."

Stewart put in the work to slim down to 280 pounds by his senior year and couldn't thank Keefer enough. The big guy who couldn't even start on the Carmel junior varsity team developed so quickly at Lawrence North that he once had an incredible 14 dunks in a single game. Already having received a full basketball scholarship to the University of Kentucky, Stewart was leading the Wildcats to a possible state title when he tragically collapsed on the court, and died later that same day due to a heart condition.

Other transfer stories have begun under cloudier settings but concluded on a positive note. Another 7-footer, Eric Montross, provides the classic "recruiting" case. Montross had *always* lived in the Lawrence North district, but he wasn't a student at Lawrence North come his freshman year of high school. Instead, he was attending a private school, Indianapolis Park Tudor.

Montross had entered kindergarten a year early because he was so intelligent for his age. Several years later, his father convinced his mother to hold Eric back a year during eighth grade, in great part because he felt Eric needed a year to "redshirt." Eric wasn't where he should have been in terms of his performance on the basketball court, according to his father. The extra year of development did wonders for Montross' basketball abilities, and by his freshman season at Park Tudor he was starting for varsity. In the summer between his freshman and sophomore years, he decided to go public—Lawrence North.

Montross said the decision was simple: "I just wanted to get back into the public school system. I came in as a sophomore and started three years at center."

His continued improvement had something to do with Dave Erwin, Keefer's chief assistant for many years, who took the awkward center under his wing, working many extra hours with him on the side. As for whether anything shady occurred to lure Montross to public school, Erwin is blunt: "Jack couldn't recruit the thirstiest horse in the world to a water trough."

In Montross' case, it's easy to see the influence of parents on a child's situation. His father, Scott, was so concerned with his son's development on the court that he held him back a year in school. Why would he also not want to send his son to one of the best basketball programs in the state—especially when it was in his backyard? Jeff Leyden, a 1993 Indiana All-Star under Keefer, agrees. "Sometimes there were 75 kids at our open gym," Leyden remembers. "There was never a time I saw Coach Keefer [try to recruit someone]. ... I think it's just that parents want the best for their kids."

Chris Hill, a 2001 Indiana All-Star, presents a different type of recruiting story. The 6-foot-3 shooting guard, who later starred at Michigan State, grew up in the Lawrence North district, but never attended Jack's summer camp because he was always on the road with his AAU team. His parents had coached track at rival Lawrence Central, so they thought of moving into that district. They also looked at private school Indianapolis Cathedral for their son before sticking with Lawrence North. "Coach Keefer was the deciding factor," Hill stressed.

Not all opposing coaches are suspicious of Keefer. Ed Siegel had many titanic battles with Keefer as the longtime coach at Pike. "We kidded each other back and forth: 'What's your recruiting budget this year?'" says Siegel. "If there was some validity [to the charge of recruiting], the IHSAA would have dug it out a long time ago. When you have a successful program, you draw kids. Are you supposed to apologize for having a successful program? A lot of [transferring] goes on in Marion County."

Ray Craft, the senior assistant commissioner at the governing Indiana High School Athletic Association (IHSAA) says requests have been made on occasion to look into things at Lawrence North. "There's no question he has had kids move in there," says Craft. "[But] we never have found any evidence [of wrongdoing]."

Former Marion coach Jack Colescott also believes Keefer sports a clean record. "I don't appreciate hearing [the charges]," Colescott says. "People accuse him of being a recruiter, but it's been the same preposterous stories. ... By his record [Keefer] can handle talent and he can coach."

Chris Hill says he loved Keefer's discipline, passion, and affection for his players. Great players saying great things about their great coach: When you have a lineage like that to build your program upon, it's fairly easy to see why kids want to play for Lawrence North, and why Jack Keefer is the envy of the block. Build it, and they will come.

Mike Conley, playing for Spiece Indy Heat, elevates for the dunk.
Photo by David Dixon

TEN

There's no doubt that Oden and Conley benefited from their off-season competition. By playing on Amateur Athletic Union (AAU) teams, they not only played in many more games during the spring and summer than they did in the high school season, but they were also able to compete against the best players in the entire country. Such competition encouraged their work ethic and expedited their improvement as players, which in turn greatly improved their impact while wearing the Lawrence North jersey.

Conley has actually won more championships in AAU ball—five, not to mention other first-place finishes at elite tournaments—than state titles. Serving as head coach, Mike Conley Sr., had shaped the Spiece Indy Heat into an awesome collection of talent in the spring of 2005. In addition to Oden and Conley, the

Heat's roster boasted top prep prospects like 6-foot-5 shooting guard Daequan Cook from Dayton, Ohio, and Indianapolis phenom Eric Gordon, whom Conley and Oden were already very familiar with from games against North Central High School.

Sporting goods executive Tom Spiece sponsored the team along with the Reebok shoe company. At the recommendation of street-wise consultant Sonny Vacarro, Reebok had spent a reported quarter-million dollars to steal the Heat from rival Nike. The sponsorship gave Vaccaro the influence to get Oden, the big draw, to play at the Reebok camp and in his Roundball Classic all-star game. More importantly, it gave Reebok the inside track to sign Oden to a lucrative shoe contract once he entered the NBA.

While Vacarro raves about the play of Oden, Conley has also impressed the executive. "If you had to describe [Conley]—in the setting he's in—he's brilliant," Vaccaro says. "He's going to be a great college player and, I think, make it in the [NBA] some day."

As incoming seniors, Greg and Mike got off to a rocky start during their final AAU go-round in the spring of 2005. Conley Sr. had started a new tournament in his old stomping grounds of Fayetteville, Arkansas. A large portion of the Conley clan was on hand for the debut of the Real Deal on the Hill Tournament, but the favored Spiece Indy Heat took it on the chin in the final game against Memphis Pump 'N Run by a surprising 76-62 margin. The Spiece Indy Heat returned to Fort Wayne, Indiana, to Spiece Fieldhouse–which features eight full courts, a large snack bar, and air conditioning among its many amenities—to take on all challengers in the 12th annual Gym Rats Run 'n' Slam All-Star Classic. They faced a formidable task to be crowned champions: winning nine games in less than three days.

The Heat debuted against the New Hampshire Players, dispatching them with ease. The triumph did little to impress Clark Francis, the veteran publisher of the Louisville-based Hoop Scoop recruiting service. Francis freely voices his opinion on anything basketball related, and as usual he was making bold statements.

"At this time," he said, "I don't think Greg Oden is the No. 1 player in his class. He needs to play harder. I would rank Kevin Durant [a 6-foot-10 power forward from Maryland] and probably Wayne Ellington [a 6-foot-4 guard from Pennsylvania] ... ahead of him."

This proclamation came despite Oden being named National Player of the Year by three publications following his junior season. Francis chalked the awards up to Oden's height, and the fact that he was surrounded by an excellent team. Later advised of Francis' comments, Conley Sr. put things into perspective: "Greg Oden *doesn't care* if he's the best player in his class. As long as he's winning, he just cares about the team."

There was little turnaround time to fret about critics, because the Heat's next game was the following day at 9:30 a.m. The Minnesota Magic went up in smoke, 78-52, and then three hours later the Heat squared off against the Los Angeles Rockfish, always a dangerous opponent. On the Heat's very first play, Oden welcomed slender 7-foot-1 sophomore David Foster into the big leagues by flashing across the lane and dunking, unceremoniously, in his face. In the third period, Oden forced his way between two defenders for an impressive reverse layup. The Heat wound up with a 68-47 triumph, their third in two days.

Then the deck of 64 teams was reshuffled, and the brackets were established for the remainder of the tournament. Up first at 5 p.m., less than three hours later, were the Inner City Players, from Oregon. Again, the Heat won with ease, jumping out to a 27-11 lead by the end of the first quarter, and winning 98-51. The starters earned plenty of rest, which they would need since the team played a fourth game that day at 9:30 p.m. The Hoosier-dominated team was going to have to win its final Saturday game against DTA Wisconsin without Cook, who by that time was attending his high school prom.

The court was ringed with people for the Heat's first big show-down of the weekend. Conley and backcourt mate Gordon more than made up for the loss of Cook, as they rained threes on the opposition to build a 33-15 lead by the end of the first quarter. Spiece won going away, 97-64, as Gordon finished with 16 points to lead the team. One day, and four games, remained to win it all.

Bright and early at 8 a.m. the following morning, the Heat groggily took to the court against the Gateway Basketball Club, from Missouri. Cook returned from his prom with a vengeance. He converted an alley-oop dunk to put the Heat on the board, then dominated the first quarter as the Heat took a commanding 27-8 lead. With the game's outcome hardly in doubt, Conley Sr. yelled "shoot that!" in Greg's direction after he passed up a 15-foot jump shot. It was no matter, though, as the Heat won a lopsided contest.

In between games, Tom Spiece strutted around the gym on stilts, wearing red- and white-striped pants with a bright red shirt. The only man in attendance capable of distracting the crowd from the 9-foot-tall man on stilts was large by normal standards. Cazzie Russell, considered by many the finest prep basketball player to come out of the Chicago area, and later a standout at both the University of Michigan and in the NBA, was taking in the action. One never knows who's going to show up at the Spiece Fieldhouse.

The 11 a.m. quarterfinal game was an emotional one for Conley Sr., because it was against the Arkansas Hawks, the team he had founded before moving to Indiana. He knew the current coaches as well as the players. Playing a methodical form of ball, The Hawks battled the Heat to an 11-11 stalemate at the end of the first eight minutes. With Oden a nonfactor on offense, the Heat eked out a 24-21 halftime lead. In the third quarter, however, the Heat awoke, smoking the Hawks in the second half on the way to a 65-45 victory. Oden's jump hook was on display, punctuated by Cook, who drove the left baseline and rammed home a spectacular dunk.

In the semifinals, the Heat squared off against the Illinois Fire, who had eliminated them a year earlier. Spiece earned revenge in a hard-fought 71-61 victory, thanks to deadly perimeter shooting from Conley, Gordon, and even Oden, who started the game by drilling an 18-footer. Next up was Cincinnati's DI Greyhounds—who had defeated the LeBron James sponsored King James Shooting Stars in the semifinals—in the tourney championship.

The Greyhounds were led by the nation's top-ranked sophomore, 6-foot-4 shooting guard O.J. Mayo, and his near-equal, 6-foot-5 Bill Walker. Mayo is a terrific shooter who is outstanding in all phases of the game. Much like the backcourt he would face for the Heat, Mayo makes the game look almost effortless. Walker, meanwhile, is an extremely aggressive player notorious for his rim-rattling dunks and tenacious rebounding. Regardless of whether the Greyhounds had the depth to match up with the Heat, their team wasn't lacking for star power. The 10 starters comprising both team's lineups were all projected to be Division I college players.

Fans sat on the floor shoulder to shoulder to be close to the action as the game tipped off. Walker surprised the Heat by sinking a three-pointer to open the game, before reverting to his typical self with a spectacular dunk as the Greyhounds jumped out to an early three-point lead. But the Heat answered with a run of their own to tilt the tables in their favor, 15-13, at the end of the first quarter. After being shut out in the first quarter, Mayo sank two threes early in the second quarter to give his team a seven-point advantage. But then Gordon took over the game for the Heat, answering with a pair of threes and four consecutive free throws during a brief stretch that enabled Spiece to take a 34-26 lead at the half.

Early in the third quarter, Oden induced some "Ohhhs" and "Ahhhs" from the crowd with a ten-foot, fadeaway jumper, and soon afterward slammed home a thunderous reverse dunk. Following an NBA-range three pointer from Conley, the Heat held a comfortable 59-46 advantage as the third quarter drew to a close. An anticlimactic fourth quarter sealed the game for the Heat, who bested a game-high 27 points from Mayo to win 77-58. Not a bad game: For $5 the crowd was treated to at least a couple potential NBA draft lottery picks battling it out.

After nine victories, the Heat were crowned champs. Their MVP—as well as the tournament's—was Conley. Holding his MVP trophy, he deferred to his teammates—saying "the whole team played real great"—just as a wise point guard should.

Two weeks later, the Heat built upon their momentum and captured the Adidas May Classic in Bloomington, Indiana—without Oden. The center's absence mattered little in the end, however, because Conley once again displayed why he's an MVP candidate each and every game.

The momentum fizzled, though, as the Heat stumbled in their next big test, the 12th annual Bob Gibbons Tournament of Champions, held on the college campuses of Duke, North Carolina, and North Carolina State over Memorial Day weekend. The Heat cruised past their first four opponents before falling, 72-68, in the quarterfinals to eventual runner-up H-Squad, from the Los Angeles area. The Heat abandoned their interior focus for an uncharacteristic outside attack. But despite 20 points from Conley, they still lost.

In early June, Oden and Conley were among 31 players selected to receive a taste of international competition in the USA Basketball Youth Development Festival at San Diego State University. Playing for the USA White team in the gold medal game, Oden shot a perfect 9-for-9 from the field, scored 21 points, and grabbed 11 rebounds as his team thumped a strong, O.J. Mayo-led USA Blue squad, 107-85, to complete a 5-0 week. Mike added six points and tied for team leadership with six assists.

Following two weeks of scrimmages with the Indiana Junior All-Stars, Oden and Conley attended the prestigious Reebok ABCD camp at Farleigh Dickinson University in New Jersey, where they went 7-0 in play. Oden shared Player of the Week honors, while both he and Conley made the senior all-star team. Once again, the Lawrence North combo outpaced Mayo's team, with Conley limiting Mayo to 3-for-13 shooting from the floor.

Just as it had for Oden and Conley at their high school, winning became second nature during AAU play. They continued their hectic summer by rejoining the Heat to win the Reebok

Breakdown Hoops Festival in Miami, Florida, in mid-July. That was but a primer for the big one: a chance to defend their AAU title in the nation's No. 1 summer tournament, the Reebok Big Time in Las Vegas, Nevada. Many of their competitors had loaded up on top talent with one goal in mind: take out the Spiece Indy Heat.

Ten games later, the Heat had become the tournament's first repeat winner in its 11-year history. They received no favors: tournament organizer Sonny Vaccaro grouped the toughest teams in the same pool to ensure that fans received an opportunity to see the best of the best tangle in the tourney. Spiece took out the New York Panthers, then the Southern California All-Stars, led by rising junior center Kevin Love. Oden was impressive in shutting down Love, but yet again it was Conley who opened eyes. West Coast basketball guru Frank Burlison saved his highest praise for Conley, who contributed 33 points, 13 assists (against just one turnover), nine rebounds, and four steals against the Panthers and California All-Stars. Burlison wondered, "Is Mike Conley the most complete—no, let's make that the best, period—point guard in the class of 2006? … It would be a chore to convince me otherwise."

In the championship game, the Heat faced off against the D1 Greyhounds again, for the second time in that tournament. It was another nail-biter, until the three-minute mark when Spiece pulled away to win, 73-67, making Mayo 0-for-the-summer against Conley and Co. Oden was spectacular in the finale, earning MVP honors after scoring 18 points, grabbing 13 rebounds, and blocking eight shots. The most telling statistic however, was the number of fouls committed by the Greyhounds' three post players in an effort to guard Oden: 15.

By the close of Spiece's summer of fun, Hoop Scoop's Clark Francis was singing a different tune. He wrote in *Basketball Times*, "The biggest winner [this summer] was Greg Oden … [who] finally lived up to his incredible potential. And, if Oden continues to play like he did this summer, then he should be well on his way toward becoming one of the great players in the history of the game." Francis also sung Conley's praise, calling him "the clutch player of the summer…who appeared to have ice in his veins."

The compliments were none too shabby, even for a pair of two-time champions in the Hoosier state.

Ohio State coach Thad Matta speaks with Oden and Conley. AP/WWP

ELEVEN

Only two other Indiana basketball teams in the state's history have won three straight championships: Franklin High in 1920-22 and Marion High in 1985-87. But Marion held the ultimate benchmark. In addition to its three straight titles, Marion could also boast that in 1985 it had gone undefeated.

The Franklin Wonder Five, as they were known, played ball in the era of the two-hand set shot, at a time when the game was noticeably different from today. The center jump was still in effect then, which meant that after each made basket, a jump ball at mid-court decided which team would gain possession of the ball. There was also no three-second-lane violation, so a player could set up camp in the lane for as long as he liked. There were, however, traveling and double-dribbling violations; but unlike in today's game, the violator was charged with a technical foul, which allowed the opposing team to shoot a free throw. And as for free throws, the team could elect anyone to shoot, regardless of whether the chosen player was the person who had been fouled.

Overall, it was a more methodical game played with a snail's pace. Guards were primarily there for defense, while forwards dominated the game on offense. The Wonder Five's tallest player stood just 6-foot-2, and the only one to start on all three title teams was 6-foot, 170-pound forward-center Robert "Fuzzy" Vandivier, an outstanding shooter, ball handler, and passer who is enshrined in the Naismith Basketball Hall of Fame.

The Marion Giants, by contrast, were a perimeter shooting team paced by standout marksmen Jay Edwards and Lyndon Jones, who both later played for Indiana University. Retired Marion coach Bill Green says hindsight has really made him appreciate just how good his Marion teams were. "I pop in an old tape once in a while," he says. "I didn't realize we were so good, because I was always on the kids all the time. We did things I don't see college kids doing."

As for undefeated teams, a few additional Indiana high schools can make that claim. Indianapolis Crispus Attucks High School, led by Hall of Famer Oscar Robertson, posted a two-year winning streak of 45 games, which included an undefeated season in 1956. Other large schools to go undefeated include South Bend Central (1957), Indianapolis Washington (1969), East Chicago Washington (1971), and Pike (2003).

As the Wildcats prepared to enter the 2005-06 season on a quest for their third straight title, they would stare down history the entire year. To avoid distraction—and the media's persistent questioning—as best as possible, the team told itself to focus on *one* championship. It was not going to face Marion High's '85 team or the Wonder Five of Franklin or The Big O's Crispus Attucks Tigers; historically speaking, all the 2005-06 Wildcats could be bothered with was the schedule ahead. Featuring tests with two elite Illinois teams and Ohio's Dayton Dunbar—which featured Oden and Conley's AAU teammate Daequan Cook— plus games against all the usual rivals like Pike, Arlington, North Central, Carmel, and Bloomington South, Lawrence North would have its hands full. It was, perhaps, the toughest schedule ever assembled by an Indiana team. And this year, the entire nation would be paying attention from start to finish. Hoosier basketball was back in a big way, and it had Oden, Conley, Coach Keefer, and the Lawrence North Wildcats to thank for that.

When Oden and Conley were not on the court with their AAU team, Spiece Indy Heat, during the spring and summer of 2005, they gave plenty of thought to their future. They visited the Wake Forest campus in the spring. After their visit, Wake Forest coach Skip Prosser called Coach Shelt and said, "We really had no plans of offering a scholarship to Greg. But when he got here, he opened the door for us and he was very polite. So we had to ask ourselves, 'What risks would we be taking? A kid like this is such a great kid, how can we not offer him? If he goes pro, he goes pro.'"

Oden was also recruited by Indiana coach Mike Davis, who was convinced of Oden's sincerity about going to college. North Carolina coach Roy Williams flew into Indianapolis to meet with Conley and Oden. So did Michigan State's Tom Izzo, Ohio State's Thad Matta, and Illinois' Bruce Weber. Matta had a leg up, having recruited Conley when he was coaching at Xavier prior to taking the Ohio State job. Now that he was at Ohio State, a major Big Ten university, Matta was prepared to make his push to get Conley *and* Oden. He showed up in Indianapolis with a carefully constructed packet of information for each of them. As part of his pitch, he also met with the players' parents and Coach Keefer, detailing to each the school's academic program, the team's weight program, and his plans for them on the basketball court. In mid-May, Conley and Oden returned the interest with a visit to the Ohio State campus.

Conley simply had to select a school, but the pressure on Oden was more complex. He was being touted as the top overall pick in the 2006 NBA draft. Would he, or wouldn't he, turn pro following his senior season? He had just been named the National High School Player of the Year, joining LeBron James as the only junior to ever receive the award. Riches awaited him. Just from a business perspective, could he turn that down? Especially when a debilitating knee or ankle injury in college could take him from future prince to immediate pauper.

But the NBA made Oden's decision for him when it reached an agreement with the players association in June 2005 that a player had to be at least 19 years old and one year removed from high school in order to be eligible for the draft. The NBA was trying to clean up its image; for every high school-to-pros superstar like Kevin Garnett and LeBron James, there were a dozen other high school kids who were overwhelmed and too immature to handle the jump to the NBA. For those players, instead of having the opportunity to develop their games in college, they were sitting on the end of the bench in the NBA, drawing huge paychecks and contributing little, if anything.

For a kid like Oden who had remained insistent on his plan to attend college, the NBA's ruling had little effect, outside of some teasing. The Lawrence North coaches kidded Oden that he had cut a secret deal with NBA commissioner David Stern so that he could live out his dream of attending college. With that pressure off his shoulders, Oden verbally agreed to attend Ohio State with his teammate Conley. It was never a given that they were a package deal, but they'd always liked the thought of going to college at the same school. At Ohio State, they would join an impressive recruiting class including a fellow member of their Spiece Indy AAU team, Daequan Cook; another highly regarded high school small forward, David Lighty, from Cleveland, Ohio; and junior college transfer Othello Hunter, a power forward. Together, the four freshmen were already being touted as the second coming of the famed "Fab Five" class at Michigan in the early '90s that included Jimmy King, Ray Jackson, and future NBA millionaires Juwan Howard, Chris Webber, and Jalen Rose.

Coach Matta, a former Butler University player, believes that the bond he built with Oden and Conley—plus Cook's early verbal commitment—made the difference in his Buckeyes beating out Wake Forest for their services. "We let them know we were going to take care of them, and that guys who come here get better," he says.

The decision to attend Ohio State was an interesting one, solely because the university was in the process of being reprimanded by the NCAA for recruiting violations incurred under the reign of their previous coach, Jim O'Brien. The NCAA ruling could have impacted the school's ability in future recruiting, or more importantly, disallowed Ohio State from participating in the NCAA tournament. Matta gave Oden and Conley a unique "escape clause" to ease their concern: In case the Buckeyes were put on probation prior to the duo's freshman season, both players' commitment to Ohio State would be voided, even after they signed their binding letter of intent. The probation did not materialize, though, and Matta's confidence paid off.

Oden and Conley's commitment to Ohio State allowed everyone at Lawrence North to breathe a collective sigh of relief. Now, everything was settled, and the focus could return to November 23, 2005, the night the Wildcats' season would begin anew.

Even though Lawrence North was the preseason No. 1 high school team in the country, their success was hardly a given. The Wildcats had suffered heavy losses from graduation. Brandon McPherson, who was named an Indiana All-Star, was gone. So was Donald Cloutier, whose inside presence augmented Oden. Also gone were two key role players, Warren Wallace and Tyler Morris. All four had received scholarships from Division I schools, and that was a lot of talent to be without.

A fifth graduate whose name was often embroiled in controversy, Zach Stewart, was gone with good riddance. As his senior season wound down, Stewart attended one of the Wildcats' open-gym sessions. There he got into a verbal confrontation with Oden that escalated to the point that Coach Etherington had to step in-between the players while they were pulled away from each other. Stewart left the gym and about a half hour later his father showed up, noticeably irate, and went after Etherington. Two players grabbed Stewart's father before any punches were thrown. That was the end for Zach Stewart: He was banned from the gym in an unceremonious end to his high school career.

Despite needing to replace a total of eight seniors, Coach Keefer was confident he had the building blocks to surround his two stars with a strong supporting cast. Brandon McDonald was returning and would step in as starting forward. Stout 6-foot-5 junior Damian Windham would be called upon to replace Cloutier. Windham was a strong rebounder who had the potential to become a scoring threat. The final piece to the starting puzzle was Qadr "Q" Owen, a 5-foot-11 defensive specialist to complement Conley in the backcourt.

While the starting line-up was sufficiently patched, the bench was of concern. Jeremy Henderson, the other Craig Middle School alumnus from the Oden-Conley team, was injured and had never fulfilled the potential he had shown in junior high school. A pair of tall freshmen, Stephan Van Treese and Chris Read, had no high school experience. Senior Evar Jones could spell Owen at guard, and Kamal Thomas was a steady back-up for Conley. But this wasn't a team that had a Tyler Morris or a Warren Wallace coming off the bench, a player who could make a sudden impact. The pressure would be on the starting five all year long to produce, remain healthy, and stay out of foul trouble.

Just as Coach Keefer had demanded Oden take on more of the offensive load last season, he told Conley he expected more offense from his point guard this year. Conley had averaged 10.8 points a game as a junior, with 5.1 assists and 3.1 rebounds. Being a little more selfish was a difficult adjustment for Conley, who long ago had flipped a switch from scorer to supplier. Keefer needed him to find a balance between the two, to keep his team's offense running smoothly, but to also be counted upon to score in bunches if necessary. "You can pretty much do what you want out there, so let's go ahead and prove it," Keefer told him. "Let's go out there and stick it to them. Let's not coast. Let's come right from the jump and put it on them."

Keefer also anointed Conley the team leader, the player who would decide the color of the warm-ups, give pregame pep talks, and take care of problems before they reached the coaches. Two years ago, he would have been too nervous and shy to take on the role. But he'd learned from teammates Penny Sargent, Stefan Routt, and McPherson; and he had grown as much emotionally as he had physically.

Of course, the focus was still on Oden, and Coach Keefer had one area in particular that he wanted to see improvement: Oden's free throw shooting. *The Indianapolis Star* did its annual pre-season feature story on Oden in November, and aptly captured the expectations heaped upon his young shoulders. One long-time high school scout called him the "Bill Russell of his era," adding that Oden was the most accomplished prep center since Lew Alcindor. Oden shrugged off the fuss. "I know I'm not there yet," he told the paper. "That motivates me to come in at 6:30 in the mornings so I *can* get there."

The paper also did the inevitable preseason story on Lawrence North's chances of winning its third straight championship. Several coaches from other schools diplomatically discussed the tough schedule Lawrence North faced and how a handful of teams were capable of defeating them on any given night. But North Central coach Doug Mitchell was more pointed. "We know we can beat them," he confidently declared. "We're 10 times better than we were last year because we can defend and rebound."

Keefer and Mitchell already were not fond of each other, both possessing an "I'd love to beat your ass" attitude about the other. Mitchell's statement to *The Indianapolis Star* placed a smile on Keefer's face; he knew he'd gotten into Mitchell's head. But Mitchell's comments also rang true for most every opposing head coach that Keefer would face that year. Every school on their schedule would be gunning for them. One team, Indianapolis Cathedral, even began practicing for its expected game against the Wildcats in that year's sectionals a full three months before the state tournament even began.

Lawrence North's fourth and final year of the Conley-Oden era began where the third had ended: at Conseco Fieldhouse. The Wildcats were part of the Keybank Classic, a trio of high school games played in front of 7,000 fans. Lawrence Central was once again the opening opponent, and the Wildcats came out determined to establish that defense was still king. Coach Keefer had preached a simple philosophy in practice: make sure the opponent doesn't get a good look at the basket, and if they miss, make certain they don't get a second shot. If Lawrence North could do those two things, everything else would take care of itself.

For the third straight year, Lawrence Central was no match for their neighbors, and the Wildcats ran away with a 62-33 win. Oden had 19 points and 15 rebounds, but it was Conley who led the team with 20 points, giving the Wildcats the kind of offensive punch that Coach Keefer had pushed him to deliver. Conley shot 5-of-8 from behind the three-point arc, and had four assists and three steals. Even more to Keefer's liking was the Wildcats' defense: Lawrence Central was held to 22-percent shooting for the game.

In their first home game of the season, Lawrence North jumped to a 16-0 lead against Brebeuf Jesuit, and ended up with a

72-49 win. Terre Haute South tried to slow down the pace against Lawrence North in the third game of the season, but they may as well have been a picket fence trying to stop a bulldozer. The Wildcats jumped out to a 23-5 lead and won 74-45. Oden and Conley combined for almost half of their team's points.

The first big test of the season came in the fifth game, an ESPN2 televised matchup between the Wildcats and Daequan Cook and his Dayton Dunbar teammates. Cook was a legitimate five-star prospect, averaging 22.6 points and 11 rebounds per game. At 6-foot-5, his leaping ability and mid-range game were his strengths, and if his outside shot was falling, he could be nearly unstoppable. Coach Shelt drove the Lawrence North staff to Dayton to scout Cook's team, and what the coaches saw on the court worried them. Dunbar was extremely talented offensively, so fast that they had no problem driving past people. They also had a 6-foot-9, 290-pound power forward named Aaron Pogue, another member of Oden and Conley's AAU team, who was a beast inside.

But the coaches did make one observation: Dunbar didn't like to play defense. They would trap opponents in the open court to try for a steal, but they had no interest in playing half-court defense. Even so, the coaches were at a loss as to how to defend against Dunbar and, especially, Cook. They finally decided to turn their attention to shutting down everyone else on the team, and take their chances with Cook.

A crowd of 9,000 fans was expected for the Tuesday night game at Hinkle Fieldhouse. What no one was expecting, however, was a mid-day snowstorm that dumped ten inches of snow on Indianapolis and shut down the highways. Coach Shelt had taken Damian Windham and back-up forward Wesley Smith to his home for a pregame dinner not long after the storm hit. Coach

Keefer called to suggest that they get started back to school. Shelt lived only four miles from Lawrence North, and his house was right off Interstate 465; he told Keefer they'd be there in a few minutes. It took Shelt 45 minutes to reach the interstate and just as he was about to turn onto the northbound ramp, a tractor-trailer coming from the other direction skidded and blocked the entire ramp.

Shelt's only choice was to get on I-465 south and go directly to Hinkle, bypassing the high school altogether. Through the traffic and the snow, they arrived only a few minutes before game time to find the gym virtually empty. Six or seven fan buses from Dayton had been turned away at the Indiana border, and few from Indianapolis tried to brave the snowstorm. There were maybe 500 people at Hinkle, and many of those were stadium workers and ESPN personnel.

Cook was a problem from the start for the Wildcats. Lawrence North put Owen on him, and Cook immediately drove into the lane and shot over him. They tried Brandon McDonald on him next, and Cook took McDonald down to the post and quickly drew two fouls on him. The answer to stopping Cook on this night may have been an unintentional elbow to the face. In the second quarter, Cook jumped for a rebound just as Oden was coming down. Oden's elbow clocked Cook in the eye, and the dazed Cook was forced to leave the game.

But Dunbar hung in without its star player, and Lawrence North was up by just three points early in the fourth quarter. The Wildcats finally broke free with a 16-3 run in the fourth quarter to win 69-54. Though Oden had faced a triple-team led by Pogue, he still wound up with 23 points, 17 rebounds, and nine blocked shots. The most encouraging aspect of the game for Oden was that he shot 9-of-10 from the free throw line, a marked improvement from the previous season. Conley scored 13 points despite playing through a stomach virus, and McDonald picked up the offensive slack with 17 points.

Oden didn't come out of the game unscathed. He was running downcourt with Pogue guarding him when another Dunbar player ran into Pogue, causing his head to smack Oden in the mouth. Oden had to have several stitches as a result, and his jaw was so swollen that he sat out the next game, which happened to be against the No. 6 team in the state: Fort Wayne Snider.

Lawrence North had already anticipated a tough game against Fort Wayne before Oden's injury. The coaches weren't sure what to expect with Oden on the bench and freshman Chris Read starting in his place. One thing was sure: Conley was now the team's primary weapon. The game was on his shoulders, and Conley responded with 26 points. The revelation, however, came in the form of McDonald, who added 20 points, shot 9-of-12 from the field, and was aggressive on defense all night. Without Oden on the court, the Wildcats not only dismissed the No. 6 team in the state, they almost doubled the score against them, 89-45.

Four days later, Lawrence North also manhandled Indianapolis Arlington. The previous year, when they'd lost to Arlington, Lawrence North had played to Arlington's strength—team speed—by putting on the press, allowing Arlington far too many transition lay-ups. After that loss, Coach Keefer told his coaches, "I've got to be a dumbass. If I ever talk about pressing Arlington again, just slap me."

The Wildcats planned to run their fast break, pound the ball inside, and play zone defense to take advantage of Arlington's lack of perimeter shooting. Coach Shelt scouted Arlington, and when he saw the line-up card, he realized that their coach, Larry Nicks, was so worried about Lawrence North's rebounding advantage that he was starting a big line-up with only one guard in the line-up who could handle the ball. Shelt went up to Keefer before the game to alert him. "Jack, I know you really don't want to press them, but there's not a ball-handler in this group, just one kid," Shelt said. "If we come out and press, it'll be over right away." Lawrence North took Shelt's advice, built an early 24-14 lead, and dominated the rest of the game to win 81-55.

Lawrence North wasn't just winning its games; it was steamrolling over its opponents. For opposing teams concerned with how to shut down both Oden and Conley, the scariest thing was the emergence of McDonald as a third offensive weapon. Against Arlington, Oden had scored 23 points, Qadr Owen and Damian Windham each scored 12, and McDonald and Conley both added 11. Playing against the national high school player of the year was one thing. But how could any team compete against *that* kind of scoring balance?

In December, Indianapolis' Southport High School hosted the Challenge of Champions Showcase. Lawrence North was in the tournament's main event against Proviso East, a Maywood, Illinois, powerhouse featuring 6-foot-11 senior center Brian Carlwell, who was signed to attend the University of Illinois. Before the game, Carlwell spoke confidently about the matchup, and even boasted to reporters that he was faster and more athletic than Oden. The Lawrence North coaches cut the story out of the newspaper, highlighted the quotes, and taped it on the wall. Just before the game, Coach Shelt went up to Oden and reminded him that Ohio State and Illinois were both in the Big Ten Conference.

"Hey, go out there and show the kid what he's going to get for the next four years," Shelt told Oden.

Carlwell was impressive: he ran the floor well; he hustled; he was on the court every minute of the game even though his team had played the night before, then had to make a three-hour bus trip to Indianapolis. He finished the game with nine points and eight rebounds. But Oden just destroyed him. Oden had had so few chances to play against legitimate big men, that no one realized he usually played better against them. He was faster, and certainly more agile, than any high school player his size. He could lean back on a tall guy, then make his spin move. When the player guarding him was just 6-foot-5, Oden couldn't do that; if he leaned back, he'd get undercut or topple over. Against Carlwell, he could use his strength to back the big man down, and his quickness to move around him. Or he could face up against Carlwell, fake a shot attempt, and drive for the dunk.

Oden's stat line by game's end was one of the best in his career: 31 points, 16 rebounds, and four blocked shots. Conley pitched in 10 points and 11 assists as Lawrence North pulled away for a 72-59 win. "It was a great challenge," Oden said after the game, noting that the coaches had put up Carlwell's quote in the locker room. "What I'm looking at now, when I think about him, is that I'm going to see him for the next four years because he's going to Illinois."

The Wildcats enjoyed a lengthy break for the Christmas holidays following their win over Proviso East. On January 3, they returned to face Franklin Central on the road. The team was off kilter from the beginning, possibly shaking off some rust from its break. When Oden picked up two early fouls and was forced to the bench, it was up to Conley to carry the offensive load. At the end of the third quarter, the Wildcats led by only three points. Just before the fourth quarter, assistant coach Joe Leonard—who coached the junior varsity team but sat on the bench during the varsity games—challenged Oden. "You're walking around with your head down," he told him. "We need somebody to play with some heart out there." Leonard emphatically made his point: if Oden moped on the court, his teammates would follow his lead. And if he played with enthusiasm and vigor, others would do the same.

Lawrence North went on a 19-2 run in the fourth quarter for a 57-38 victory, with Conley scoring 23 points. After the game, astonished Franklin Central coach Mark James told reporters, "It was the roadrunner: beep, beep ... they're gone."

Lawrence North entered the annual Marion County Tournament undefeated, with a record of 9-0. Even though the Wildcats had lost so much talent from last year's squad, many fans and critics alike were ready to declare that this year's team might be even better than its predecessor. Lawrence North was averaging 72.3 points a game, seven points higher than the previous season. And Oden had upped his average to 22.6 points per game, largely on his improved free throw shooting. While Conley's assists average was holding steady with his junior numbers, he'd upped his scoring average from 10.8 points per game to 17.4 as a senior.

Coach Keefer told *The Indianapolis Star* that he hadn't expected to be unbeaten at this juncture of the season. "We have a very young team around the three veterans, and I thought it would take the bench and two new starters time to adjust," he said. "But we've been playing such good defense that it's made us competitive right away."

Going into the tournament, Lawrence North was holding opponents to only 47.4 points a game, lower than their average in either of the two prior seasons. "I think our defense is better [than the previous two championship teams]," Keefer told the newspaper. "We didn't have a good offensive game [against Franklin Central], but we held them to 38 points. You're not going to lose very often when people score in the 30s. That defense enabled us to struggle on offense but still beat a team by 19 points."

However, struggling offensively in the county tournament would get the Wildcats eliminated, as their competition would steeply improve. Their championship aspirations were about to be sternly tested. After taking care of Ben Davis 81-40 to open tourney play, they were due to play Pike (7-1) in the second game. If they won that game, a likely matchup loomed with Coach Mitchell's North Central High (8-1).

Pike was ranked No. 3 in the state, its only loss coming at the hands of Bloomington South. Pike also had handed North Central, ranked No. 6, its lone loss of the year. But Pike was vulnerable because, word was, their tallest player had been kicked off the team and they had no remaining post players. Playing at home, Lawrence North got its usual offensive burst at the start of the game when Conley opened things with a three-point shot and the Wildcats built a 7-0 lead. Pike closed the gap with a 9-4 run before Conley ignited an 11-0 Lawrence North run with another three-point shot. By halftime, the Wildcats had almost doubled the score, 40-24.

They built their lead to over 20 points late in the third quarter before Pike, using a press, started a run to climb back into the game. Lawrence North held on for a 73-60 win, the team's smallest margin of victory all season. After the game, the Wildcat coaches were taken aback when the two teams met at half-court to shake hands and Pike coach Larry Bullington, with more than a little cockiness in his voice, said, "I'll see you guys in February."

Coach Keefer was not happy about Pike's comeback, and kept the team in the locker room long after the game to tell them he expected more from a team that aspired to win its third consecutive state championship. "I thought we were sloppy," Keefer told reporters. "We got up and let up. A good team would have put them away in the fourth, and we let them fight back. ... I was a little disappointed."

Conley glumly echoed Keefer. "We're not there yet, a state-championship type of team," he said. "We're real upset with ourselves. Even though we won, the win doesn't matter much to us. We want to get better."

Keefer did, however, reserve praise for his senior point guard for breaking the Pike runs with clutch shooting. "He's taken more of a responsibility for what goes on," Keefer told *The Indianapolis Star*. This is a kid that is one of the finest guards in the nation, and we kept saying, 'We expect more out of you. We don't want a 10-point game. We want more.' And he's done it."

Next up in the county tournament was a rematch with Franklin Central, and this time the Wildcats didn't come out flat. Behind a patient offense and a swarming defense, Lawrence North broke out to a large first-quarter lead. Although the final score was almost identical to their previous meeting, this game was an easy win that allowed Keefer to rest his starters.

As expected, for the championship the Wildcats faced North Central. It was time to see if Coach Mitchell's proclamation of confidence would hold up on court. Keefer's point of focus was diminishing the scoring ability of Eric Gordon. Contain Gordon—North Central's only real threat—and the Wildcats would win the game. Over the summer when the Wildcats were working out one day in the weight room, Keefer shared his opinion on North Central with his assistant coaches. "You know, all these accolades, all these awards, they're great," Keefer said. "Not allowing Josh McRoberts to ever win the sectional, that makes me happy. But if I can keep Eric Gordon from winning the state championship, I'll feel satisfied."

More than 5,000 people squeezed into the Southport gymnasium to watch the state's three best players vie for the championship of Marion County. It was a physical game inside. North Central's 6-foot-7 center, Adnan Hodzic, leaned on Oden the entire game. Coach Keefer gave McDonald the chore of trying to stop Gordon, instructing him to make Gordon work for every shot. The last thing Lawrence North wanted was for Gordon to get easy baskets.

The game was tight for three quarters. Lawrence North received a huge game from Damian Windham. The junior forward had quietly gained confidence and had begun to make his presence felt as a big-time rebounder and clutch scorer. With Oden facing constant double teams, Windham torched North Central for 15 points, most of them lay-ups and lay-ins off offensive rebounds.

Still, North Central was able to hang around 55-50 as the fourth quarter started. That's when Lawrence North went into its roadrunner mode; a 14-2 run allowed the Wildcats to pull away. Conley started it with a three-point shot, and Oden followed with three dunks as the Wildcats held North Central to just five points in the final quarter to win 78-55. Oden finished the game with 23 points and 12 rebounds; Conley also scored 23 points and collected nine rebounds; and McDonald held Gordon to a modest 20 points on poor 5-for-14 shooting.

The Wildcats had a peculiar postgame ritual: In the locker room, that game's most outstanding player was awarded an odd trophy—a sledgehammer. The hammer, which had belonged to Keefer's grandfather, represented a player's devotion to giving his all. It was an idea that sprang from a T-shirt that read, "You can be the hammer or you can be the nail." The sledgehammer represented toughness, and on this night, Keefer had it fetched from the locker room and brought to the bench with 35 seconds left in the game. This time the hammer belonged to the team, symbolizing a job well done in nailing the door shut on North Central.

But though he celebrated with the sledgehammer, Coach Keefer wasn't thrilled with his team's performance in the victory. North Central had outrebounded the Wildcats. At the next practice, Keefer posted Lawrence North's record as 12-1. When the players asked him what that meant, Keefer lit into them. "That game counts as a loss," he said. "We got outrebounded. There's no way that should happen. We've got a 7-footer, the No. 1 big kid in the country. We've got another kid who's 6-foot-5, and we've got Mike Conley. We don't get outrebounded. That's how you get beat, when you get beat rebounding. So that game counts as a loss."

Keefer wanted his players to keep the team's goals in mind, and not grow to accept bad habits. When they wrote out their goals for the season at the beginning of the year, winning the county tournament was not on the list. Nor was going undefeated. The list was actually very short. One item. Win State. Period.

The sight of a sledgehammer on the Lawrence North bench didn't further endear the Wildcats to Coach Mitchell. The North Central coach returned the favor when the Wildcats traveled to his gym just five days later for a nationally televised game on ESPN2. Lawrence North received just 200 tickets to the game—all far from courtside. The nosebleed seats would ensure that Wildcat fans would have little impact on the game. Even the wives of the coaching staff were seated high above courtside, and the coaches were not happy about it, especially Etherington and Shelt. The generally accepted protocol was that even if the home team couldn't take care of anybody else, it took care of the opposing coaching staff's family. No matter what, they would have good seats because the home team's coach understood and respected the sacrifices that a coach's family has to make each season. To complicate matters more, Oden's father and other relatives had traveled from Buffalo, New York, to watch Greg play.

North Central might have been better served letting sleeping dogs lie. On top of the ticket situation, Coach Mitchell had been quoted in the paper as saying Eric Gordon was the best player in the state. Not the best junior in the state, not the best guard; the best *player*.

Lawrence North made its own statement on the court. Oden proved without a doubt he was the best player in the gym. He scored 33 points, amassed 12 rebounds and four blocked shots, and shot 7-of-8 from the free throw line. Gordon had 26 points for North Central, but most of those came in garbage time. While Oden scored 23 first-half points and was 9-of-10 from the field, Gordon was again shut down by McDonald and held to 2-of-11 shooting. Lawrence North had doubled the score at halftime, 38-19, and thoroughly dominated the boards. Gordon got hot in the second half as North Central staged a comeback to pull to within 58-49 early in the fourth quarter. But Conley took over the game, scoring a bucket and hitting Oden with a pass for a dunk to put a stop to the run. The Wildcats pulled away to win 78-59.

Lawrence North was now 14-0 for the season—or 13-1, as far as Coach Keefer was concerned. Those wondering where this Wildcat team would rank in the elite history of Indiana high school basketball would be answered emphatically if the Wildcats could run the table on the season. A perfect record would give them 29 wins, which when tacked onto the 16-game win streak they ended the previous season on, would give them a total of 45 straight wins, tying them with the 1956 Crispus Attucks. No other team in Indiana history could boast of three straight championships, an undefeated season, and a 45-game win streak.

Lawrence North was well aware of that fact. When a team has a chance of breaking a longtime high school basketball record in the state of Indiana, people tend to take notice. As Keefer had preached the year before, his Wildcats were defending, and defining, their legacy. They were bidding to become the greatest high school team in the history of Indiana. Tie that win streak, and immortality would be theirs.

The 2005-06 Wildcats celebrate their state championship. Photo by David Dixon

TWELVE

Lawrence North wasn't just winning games during the 2005-06 campaign, it was blowing out such rivals as Arlington and North Central as if they were junior high teams. Pike and Proviso East had each come within 13 points of defeating the Wildcats, but that was the closest anyone had gotten to taking out the defending state champs. For opponents of the Wildcats, the unthinkable was becoming obvious: the only team that could beat Lawrence North was Lawrence North. Opponents had to hold out hope that they caught them on a severe off night, or else that Oden and Conley would get stuck in traffic on their way to the game.

Against Warren Central on January 24, the Wildcats built an overwhelming 27-5 first-quarter lead and coasted to a 69-38 win to improve to 15-0 on the season. When Coach Keefer was asked after the game about the possibility of going undefeated, he pretended that his team knew nothing about Oscar Robertson's famed 45-game win streak at Crispus Attucks High. "They don't even know what you're talking about, probably, although they did meet Oscar once," Keefer told *The Indianapolis Star*. "We just don't talk in those terms. … I guess I'm like [Indianapolis Colts coach Tony] Dungy: I go for what's next in line. You've got to play every game to win."

As if on cue, Center Grove proved Keefer's remarks wise when it threw something new at Lawrence North: a bruising, physical game that went beyond the realms of decency. The Trojans tore a page out of Arlington's playbook with their intimidation tactics, but then ramped up the intensity twofold. Playing rough, contact basketball was Center Grove's style of play, but in Lawrence North's mind, they took it way too far. Going into the game, the two coaching staffs had a good relationship. But that was suddenly in flux.

The last time the two teams had met, almost exactly a year ago, the Wildcats had more than doubled the Trojans' score, 89-44, and coach Cliff Hawkins was determined not to see a repeat. Center Grove came out very aggressive and was hitting from behind the three-point line. For their efforts, they were down just 14-12 at the end of the first quarter. Oden was being smothered inside; Center Grove's defenders were hanging on his arms in an attempt to keep him from touching the ball. Oden was used to such treatment, but the Trojan defenders were also trying to undercut him, and that wasn't okay.

The game almost turned into a melee in the second quarter when Oden pushed away from Center Grove's James Nussbaum, who was clinging to him. Nussbaum fell to the floor as though he'd been hit with a karate chop. On its next possession, Center Grove was pushing the ball upcourt when Conley stole the ball and darted to the Wildcat goal to try for an uncontested dunk. But Nussbaum had no intention of allowing Conley an easy two points. He ran up behind Conley, grabbed him by the neck, and threw him down, almost sending him into a concrete wall 10 feet away.

Qadr Owen ran down the court to protect his teammate, and Coach Etherington raced out across the half-court line to pull him away. All the while, Etherington was screaming at the officials to call a technical foul on Nussbaum. Coach Shelt responded by pulling Ehterington back to the Wildcat bench; it was illegal for a coach to leave the coaching box, as Etherington had done in the heat of the moment. Meanwhile, off to the side, Coach Hawkins was yelling out to the officials, "We're not going to back down from those guys! We're not going to back down!"

Lawrence North coaches couldn't believe that Hawkins was trying to defend that kind of thuggish play. It was the worst foul Coach Shelt had ever witnessed in a high school game, and he yelled back at Hawkins, "That's bullshit, Cliff!"

When things finally calmed down, the referees huddled together to discuss a penalty. The lead official then came over to Etherington and politely asked him to leave the game. Nussbaum, however, was allowed to continue playing. Conley sank both free throws, and the game continued its physical ways. In the fourth quarter, Lawrence North shifted into overdrive, going on a 20-5 run marked by several emphatic Oden dunks, Conley's crisp passes, and three-pointers by Owen and Brandon McDonald. The Wildcats survived the brutal battle to bury the Trojans, 76-55.

After the game, Conley shrugged off the play that sent him to the deck. "I anticipated him staying back and he just came out of nowhere," Conley said of Nussbaum. "I was scared, because I didn't know what was going on. I was just hoping I didn't hurt anything when I hit the ground. I was cool. I'm fine, [just] bumps and bruises like every game."

The Lawrence North coaches sought out the referee team after the game to discuss the call. One referee motioned to Shelt, mentioned his profanity-laced outburst, and said, "I probably should have thrown you out, too."

Shelt nodded his head. "You know what?" he replied. "You're probably right. I agree. I can't argue with you about that. But what does it take as a player to get thrown out of a game if you don't get thrown out for something like that?"

The referee thought for a moment, then nodded *his* head. "You're right," he said.

The coaches also sought out Hawkins to discuss what had happened, and everything seemed smoothed over until they read his quotes in the morning paper. Hawkins said Oden had hit Nussbaum in the head with an elbow on the previous play. Then, to their astonishment, he excused the intentional foul. "I think he was just trying to hustle," Hawkins said of Nussbaum. "My goodness, if they're going to win the state championship, they're going to have somebody make a harder foul than that. Mike Conley's going to Ohio State, he can handle that."

Coach Shelt had grown up in Indiana and seen a lot of Big Ten basketball. The conference is known for its physical play, yet he'd never seen a foul like that. "I don't know what basketball Cliff's been watching, but in college they'll throw you out and they may throw the coach out, too," Shelt said. "You don't teach basketball like that. There's a limit to how physical you play it, and he crossed the line. Center Grove was trying to hurt us. Center Grove's administration and parents, they should be appalled. That is fake toughness. That's not real toughness to club somebody from the back. That's cowardice."

The game was a wake-up call for the Lawrence North players. They were fine with being a marked team, but now they had to be sure to watch their backs.

During the 2003-04 season, Lawrence North was given an uncomfortable surprise for their game at Carmel High School: Carmel had removed the padded chairs from the visitor's bench and replaced them with non-padded chairs. This time around, the Wildcats had padded seating, but they didn't have Coach Etherington, who had to sit out the game as a penalty for being thrown out of the previous game.

Carmel had two gunners from outside, guards Jake Kelly and Brett Finkelmeier, and decided to try to draw Oden away from the basket by playing a slowdown game and utilizing a perimeter attack focused on three-point shots. For a while, it worked; at half-time, the Wildcats were up by just four points.

In the locker room, Coach Keefer made adjustments to try to dig the Wildcats out of their rut. Kelly was forced out of the game with a sprained ankle in the first quarter, so Keefer had his defense focus on stopping Finkelmeier. It worked; the Wildcats were never able to make one of their patented runs, but they did slowly pull away for a 68-49 win.

The Wildcats then traveled to Ben Davis, which had fallen to Lawrence North 81-40 in the county tournament earlier that season. One of the referees working the game was retiring after a long stint in stripes, and Coach Keefer had everyone on the team sign a ball for him. Lawrence North started the game playing a 2-3 zone defense because Keefer wasn't happy with the team's zone play, and he wanted them to work on it in game conditions.

Ben Davis kept it close for a half. But early in the fourth quarter the Wildcats increased their lead to 26 points on the strength of Oden's career-high 38 points, and Coach Keefer pulled the starters. The Giants made a run, eventually whittling down the lead to 10 points at the buzzer.

After the game, when Coach Keefer went to shake the hand of Ben Davis coach Scott White, White popped off. "Well, maybe if I give the official a signed ball before the game, we'll have a chance at winning," he snapped. Keefer was dumbfounded. After all, this was a team the Wildcats had defeated by 41 points on a neutral court. And he had pulled his starters early in the fourth quarter to prevent another massacre. It was apparent that some opposing coaches were tired of losing to the Wildcats and didn't mind communicating their frustrations in person.

The next day, Lawrence North boarded a bus to Chicago to play defending Illinois state champ Glenbrook North in the McDonald's City-Suburban Showdown. Road trips like this provided the Lawrence North team with a time to bond. They took in the sights of downtown Chicago and enjoyed a meal together at an ESPN Zone restaurant. For many Wildcats, it was their first taste of Chicago. Oden made a point to keep the window shades open in his hotel room so he could gaze at the bright lights of the city.

Their game against Glenbrook was part of a double-header at Northwestern University's Welsh-Ryan Arena, and had been sold out for more than a week. Once again, this was a matchup that pitted star against star. But in this instance, the opposing star was not a big man, but a guard. The Spartans were led by Duke recruit Jon Scheyer, a 6-foot-5 shooting guard who was the most celebrated high school player in Illinois, averaging 32 points a game.

But in Coach Keefer's mind, of course, this was a matchup of two talented *teams*. Lawrence North was ranked No. 1 in the country by *Sports Illustrated* and No. 5 by *USA Today*; Glenbrook North, from Chicago's wealthy North Shore, was 20-1 and ranked No. 12 by *USA Today*. The Spartans figured to be a tough challenge for the Wildcats. Scheyer was a lethal shooter who had once scored 21 points in only 75 seconds. His team was fundamentally sound and played an up-tempo style. But the game was to be played on a college-sized court, which was 10 feet longer than high school regulation. The added length might tire out both teams in a fast-paced game, and the Lawrence North coaching staff thought that would work to their advantage simply because of their deeper bench. The Wildcats came up with a simple game plan: wear Scheyer out so that he'd be too tired to hurt them in the second half. Lawrence North would play man-to-man defense and rotate a trio of players to guard him: Conley, McDonald, and Owen.

A record crowd of 8,500 squeezed into the arena to watch their hometown hero come out blazing in the first quarter. Scheyer scored Glenbrook's first eight points, showcasing a variety of moves. But the Wildcats weren't swayed; as Keefer always said, one player can't beat a team. Led by Oden and Conley, Lawrence North matched Scheyer point for point, and then topped him. By halftime, the Wildcats were up 14 points. The margin was impressive, especially considering that Oden had lost a contact lens in the second quarter, forcing him to play for a while with just one eye in focus.

In the second half, Scheyer's legs had turned to jelly, and by the closing minutes of the third quarter he was so winded that he'd stopped looking for his shot. Scheyer scored just one basket in the first 11 minutes of the second half, and Lawrence North easily pulled away, winning 79-61. Oden led Lawrence North with 31 points on 12-of-19 shooting, and Conley pitched in 24 points, shooting 10-of-18 from the field. Scheyer bested his season average by one in scoring 33 points in a losing cause.

After the game, Trojans head coach David Weber was both gracious and effusive in his comments, particularly in talking about Conley. "Oden, obviously, his size is a factor, but Conley is the best player we've seen," Weber told *The Indianapolis Star*. "We had no answer for him."

Coach Weber was hardly alone in that regard.

The first of Lawrence North's three remaining regular-season games was against one of the few teams—Bloomington South—that could claim a victory over the Wildcats in the Oden-Conley era. The Panthers were 15-3 on the season, including a win over Pike. More worrisome to the coaching staff was that the game was being played in Bloomington with a questionable group of referees. On the Wildcats' last trip to Bloomington—a loss in 2004—the Panthers had shot over 40 free throws in the game and held a distinct advantage as a result. Coach Etherington had checked on the refs this time, and none of the ones hired to work this game had even applied to work in the sectionals, where the state's best referees were selected to work. If a referee wasn't trying to reach the postseason, what incentive did he have to call a fair game?

Officiating aside, Lawrence North coaches had another problem on their hands that was more worrisome: Oden was nursing an injury. He had sat out of all of the team's practices leading up to the game. Coach Keefer told the press it was because he wanted to get the team conditioned to playing without Oden, since he figured the center would be hit with foul trouble against Bloomington South. But Oden had actually injured his ankle, and Keefer didn't want anyone to know. He also hoped to apply a little pregame psychological pressure in the hope that the Wildcats might get a better-called game this time around.

It didn't work. In the junior varsity game, Bloomington South shot 21 free throws to Lawrence North's two. In the varsity game, the officiating wasn't much better. Bloomington South was actually called for twice as many fouls as Lawrence North. But Oden was sent to the bench with four fouls early in the second half, and then Coach Keefer was whistled for a technical foul for protesting the call. Once Oden returned to the game in the fourth quarter, he and Conley led the team on a run to steer them to a 10-point win, 60-50.

After that experience, the Wildcats almost welcomed their next game against Pike. Sure, Coach Bullington had challenged the Wildcats after their first meeting in the Marion County Tournament, telling Coach Keefer after the game, "See you in February." But Pike didn't play dirty. The Wildcats knew they'd get a fair game—Pike's best against their best. And that was the way Keefer liked it.

As with most meetings between these two teams, this was a hyped game, pitting the No. 1-ranked Wildcats against the second best team in the state. Pike featured the state's most explosive offense, averaging over 77 points a game; Lawrence North had one of the toughest defenses in the state, holding opponents to 50 points a game. Keefer preached defense, and on this night he would see if his teachings were the gospel truth.

It was understood going in that Pike was going to press; the Red Devils tallest starter was only 6-foot-4, and they had to keep Lawrence North from setting up their regular offense if they had any hope of winning the game. That meant applying pressure in the open court, putting the onus on the Wildcat guards to break the press. Lawrence North was successful at first, jumping out to a 10-0 lead. Pike was running a 2-2-1 press, and Lawrence North utilized Oden's height advantage and installed him as a stationary passer to break the press, allowing the Wildcats some uncontested lay-ups in transition. But Lawrence North altered its approach as the game progressed, slowing the tempo down and turning the ball over. Pike was able to claw its way back into the game, and give Lawrence North its first real test of the year.

With 2:02 left in the game, Pike hit a three-point shot to pull to within one point, 65-64. But Conley and Oden showed their senior mettle and willed the Wildcats to victory on the heels of a 9-2 run over the final two minutes. Conley hit two free throws and a jump shot, then Oden sank two more free throws as the Wildcats edged the Red Devils, 74-67. Oden finished the game with a spectacular stat line: 35 points on 12-of-12 shooting from the floor and 11-of-13 shooting from the foul line. Conley backed him up with 17 points, seven assists, and six rebounds, one more than Oden. It was the smallest margin of victory for the Wildcats since their four-point defeat of Carmel the previous season.

Before the final home game of the year—Senior Night for Oden and Conley—the McDonald's All-America team was announced. Both Conley and Oden had earned the distinguished honor. But there wasn't much celebration in-house because the Wildcats were preoccupied with re-establishing their dominance after the struggle with Pike. Terre Haute North was a tough matchup. The last thing Keefer wanted was to lose for the first time that season on what should have been a happy night for his seniors.

The Patriots came out playing a triangle defense that left Oden guarded by a zone of three players. Their philosophy for the game was obvious: don't get blown out. The previous year, the Patriots had been manhandled by the Wildcats in the last game of the regular season, which had destroyed their confidence going into the state tourney. They might not beat Lawrence North this time around either, but they were determined not to get run off the court again.

Coach Keefer was animated on the sideline, imploring defensive intensity from his players; especially on a "diamond press" he wanted the team to work on for inbounds plays. When Terre Haute successfully inbounded on two straight plays, he called a time-out to demand that his players stop the next inbound pass. And they did. All told, the Wildcats forced 18 turnovers, and though Terre Haute succeeded in keeping the game relatively close, the 46-32 outcome was never in question.

The regular-season finale featured plenty of exclamation points for Lawrence North. The Wildcats completed an undefeated regular season for the first time in the school's 30-year history. During the Conley-Oden era, the Wildcats had never lost at home, going 34-0. And beating Terre Haute North also meant that Conley, Oden, and fellow senior McDonald had made it through their entire high school career unbeaten in Metropolitan Interscholastic Conference games. The eight-team conference featured North Central, who had beaten the Wildcats twice in that span. But both losses came in non-conference games during the Marion County Tournament.

But none of those achievements really mattered at the moment. On the dry erase board in the locker room, someone had written a large "7" in green ink. Seven was the number of games Lawrence North had to win in order to three-peat. Seven was the number that led to *one*, one more championship.

In their last practice before the beginning of the state tournament, Coach Keefer talked to the team about dealing with the pressure of the moment. "I want you to play with instinct," he told his players. "I don't want you out there thinking. If you're a thinking ballplayer, you're not any good. We do things over and over so that it becomes instinct. If you catch the ball and you're open, you should shoot it. You shouldn't catch the ball thinking, 'Oh, should I shoot it?'" Aggression was something his team had thrived on all season long. They would need it in spades if they were going to achieve their preseason goals.

The Wildcats opened tournament play against nemesis Arlington at Arsenal Technical High School on the eastside of Indianapolis. Outside the gym, television trucks prepared for a statewide broadcast, while a horde of reporters and media members swarmed the gym's insides. Hoosier hysteria was back, indeed.

The Knights employed three tactics that had worked in their defeat of Lawrence North the previous season: pressuring Conley in an attempt to force him out of his rhythm; playing a slowdown offense; and utilizing a zone defense. Despite Keefer's best efforts, Lawrence North came out tight, and things only worsened when Conley picked up his third foul early in the second quarter and had to go to the bench. Evar Jones and Kamal Thomas held the offense steady in his absence, but the Wildcats hardly had the game in hand at the half. The Knights trailed by just six points, 20-14.

But in the second half, Arlington went to a man-to-man defense, and Lawrence North exploited it, sending the ball into the paint to Oden. In the fourth quarter, the Wildcats found a higher gear and bolted past Arlington thanks to a 13-2 run that gave them a 20-point lead and finally put the game out of reach for the Knights. Oden had a couple of spectacular dunks in the game, including one alley-oop dunk on a pass from Owen that bounced off the backboard. However, on another dunk, Oden came down awkward after getting tangled up with an Arlington player. As he was falling face-first toward the floor, he extended his hands to brace his fall, and injured the wrist of his shooting arm in the process.

Three days later, Lawrence North returned to Tech High School to play Indianapolis Manual. Again, the Wildcats came out with a lack of intensity. It was as if the Wildcats were exerting the minimum effort required, storing up the excess energy for bigger games down the road. Coach Keefer was so frustrated by his team's play that he pulled the starters out of the game in the second quarter and put in the bench. Instead of Oden and Conley and Windham, the Wildcats were playing their freshmen and reserves. At halftime, Keefer laid down the law. "Hey, we can't have that," he told his players. "It shouldn't take a loss to get you motivated. If you lose now, you're done."

Keefer got his message across—Lawrence North went on to win by 30 points. "I didn't think our starting group had the energy we always ask of them," Keefer said after the game. "The kids we put in did well defensively and added the energy we needed."

The next night, Lawrence North crushed Warren Central by 25 points to win the sectional. Their defense caused the Warriors fits, and for the third straight game the Wildcats' opponent had failed to score better than 42 points. Lawrence North seemed to have regained their stride just in time for regional play.

And once again, the road to the state championship would go through Pike.

The previous two years, Lawrence North had played in the 10 a.m. game in their first regional contest. The advantage to playing the early game was that the coaches could send the players home to rest before returning for the nightcap. Meanwhile, the coaches could scout the following game and mentally prepare for the victor.

However, this year the Wildcats were playing in the later game at noon. That meant less time to rest, and Lawrence North needed all the rest it could get since Conley had sprained an ankle during the previous weekend's sectional. The regional double-header was always the roughest on guards, who were depended upon to sprint up and down the court. The start time wasn't doing Conley's ankle any favors.

Lawrence North's opponent for the noon game was the Carmel Greyhounds. Though Carmel had posted a modest 17-7 record that year, they were still to be feared. Coached by Mark Galloway, a former hard-nosed guard from Bethel College, Carmel was a sharp-shooting perimeter team making its deepest trip into the brackets since Galloway's arrival. They had knocked off North Central the week prior to capture the sectional crown.

The Wildcats had easily handled the Greyhounds in their earlier meeting that season. But one of Carmel's primary scorers, 6-foot-6 guard Jake Kelly, had left that game in the first quarter with an ankle injury. Kelly and fellow guard Brett Finkelmeier were three-point specialists, and if either got hot from outside, then Lawrence North would have serious problems. "We know our work is cut out for us," Galloway told *The Indianapolis Star* before the game. "They're talking about making history, but so are we. If we can knock off the No. 1 team in the country and get a shot at the No. 2 team in the state [Pike], what a great day of basketball that would be."

Though March 11 was a cold and rainy day in Indianapolis, the streets surrounding Hinkle Fieldhouse quickly grew congested with anxious basketball fans. The Lawrence North school bus pulled into the parking lot at about 10 a.m. and parked in the back by a garage door entrance, allowing the team to enter the gym in the shadow of the surrounding hysteria. The Wildcats took their designated seats behind the basket to watch the first game, Pike against Franklin.

Despite starting out 7-10 and finishing with a mediocre 14-11 record, Franklin had gotten hot during the state tournament and won its sectional. Pike, on the other hand, was a perennial powerhouse with a 20-3 record—two of those losses coming at the hands of Lawrence North. Since Indiana had switched to the four-class system in 1997, Pike had won three state titles and finished second another time. A deep run in the state tourney was nearly a given for Pike.

Franklin managed to keep the game close for three quarters before Pike pulled ahead on the contributions of its two starting junior guards, Reece Cheatham and Jeff Teague, who scored a combined 38 points in the Red Devils' victory. Cheatham nailed

5-of-6 threes to ignite Pike's perimeter attack. Overall, the team hit 10-of-14 threes, and that kind of outside shooting worried the Lawrence North coaches. But first they had to deal with Carmel. Containing their three-point shooters would serve as ample practice for defending Pike.

As the Lawrence North team hit the court, rowdy Franklin fans—whose team had just been eliminated—greeted them with the chant, "Ree-crui-ters! Ree-crui-ters! Ree-crui-ters!" Halfway through the Wildcats' warm-up drills, the Pike team set up camp courtside and watched intently. Pike hadn't defeated Lawrence North since beating them twice during Oden and Conley's freshman season. This year, they wanted to be responsible for sending Lawrence North to the showers.

The Carmel players, warming up across the court, were determined to get first crack at that distinction. But to do so, they would have to get creative on the defensive end. Their tallest player was only 6-foot-6, and they would assign the job of guarding Oden to 6-foot-5 Jordan Brewer. Even though they had played Lawrence North close for a half the last time they'd played, Carmel looked like a high school team about to take on a college team. The size difference was that pronounced: the Wildcats had five players 6-foot-6 or taller.

Five minutes before game time, both teams retreated back to their respective locker rooms. Three minutes later, the Wildcats re-emerged to do a final round of lay-ups. When the game horn sounded, Carmel was still in the locker room, delaying the introductions for a couple of minutes while officials waited for them to finally come out. Possibly they were playing subtle mind games with the Wildcats; or maybe they were stalling for more time, hoping that some unforeseen strategy would expose itself to lead them to a monumental victory.

The Greyhounds hung with the Wildcats for the first quarter thanks to Kelly, who had scored all eight of Carmel's points. But Lawrence North had managed to throw Carmel off its offensive game with one simple adjustment: by jumping picks, they forced Carmel's point guard to dribble with his weak hand, making it difficult for him to go in his preferred direction to set up the offense. The minor disturbance packed a major punch as Carmel struggled to find a comfort zone on offense. Owen was doing a fabulous job neutralizing Finkelmeier.

Meanwhile, the Greyhounds were doubling down on Oden, who was locked in a heated physical battle with Brewer. The Carmel defender was leaning his weight into Oden as the big man struggled for position on the block. Baskets weren't coming too easy for Greg on this afternoon, but his supporting cast was making Carmel pay the price for paying so much attention to one player. Early in the game, McDonald threw a perfect ally-oop pass to the stocky-yet-quick Windham for a dunk. The Wildcats were showing off their offensive depth.

By halftime, Lawrence North was up 21-10, and Kelly was still the only Carmel player to score. The Wildcats continued to pull ahead in the second half, suffocating the Greyhound offense in perhaps the Wildcats strongest defensive performance of the Oden-Conley era. The final score, 47-22, surely sent a shiver up Pike's spine, as they took in the whooping from their courtside seats. Carmel—which shot 49.8 percent during the season—was limited to just 18-percent shooting against the Wildcats.

If Pike had an answer for Lawrence North's stranglehold on the title, the state of Indiana would find out shortly. The nightcap was set: Devils versus Wildcats, No. 1 against No. 2.

Jordan Brewer had transferred from Pike to Carmel following his freshman season; had he remained a Red Devil, his presence would have given Pike an entirely different dimension in facing Lawrence North. But word on the street was that if you were a big man, you didn't want to play for Pike, because they didn't pass the ball down to the post. Pike coach Larry Bullington had built his foundation on guards and outside shooting. Without an intimidating post player, Bullington had no go-to man to guard Oden. His strategy reflected such a predicament: play Oden one-on-one, roll the dice, and make sure that the rest of the Wildcat team didn't beat him.

When the two teams had met at Lawrence North in February, the Wildcats had eked out a seven-point win, providing Pike with a ray of hope for the future. If they could play Lawrence North close on the Wildcats' home court, beating them on neutral ground was definitely within the realm of possibility. The Wildcat coaching staff recognized that fact, and paid Coach Bullington a compliment: Over the next two weeks, they dedicated a part of every practice to attacking Pike's offensive tendencies. Their focus: defending the double-screen around the arc, which the Red Devils used to great effect to create spacing for their talented guards to operate and get open looks on the perimeter. Lawrence North was about to find out if it had been time well spent.

The atmosphere inside Hinkle had all the frenzy of a NCAA Sweet 16 game. The Lawrence North high school band filled up an entire section of seats, pumping the fieldhouse full of hard-driving R&B classics. The Wildcats stormed the gym, jogging a lap around the court before splitting into two lines for a lay-up drill. Pike's players followed, forming a line on their end of the court to shoot three-point shots. They were making their intentions known: the Red Devils would live and die by the three.

Pike pounced early, building a quick lead on the strength of their full-court press. But Oden converted a lay-up, and then Conley followed with a three-pointer to give Lawrence North a tiny, four-point cushion, which shortly ballooned into an 18-9 lead. But Pike wasn't about to give in. Teague challenged Oden inside, tossing up a rainbow that sailed just over Oden's outstretched hand for two points. Cheatham joined in the Pike counterpunch with a string of threes. Then midway through the second quarter, Pike made a sudden change in tactics and went to a five-guard line-up. Their intention was to lure Oden out to the top of the key, leaving the lane free for lay-ups. It was a strategy that opposing coaches had been trying for four years. And it didn't work. Oden, who had been pushed in practice to guard smaller, quicker players, was fast enough to stay with Pike's guards.

In addition, Keefer had devised a special defense simply titled "The Wildcat" to combat such a strategy. When a team forced Oden out of the paint, they simply made a switch on the player Oden was guarding in order to keep him near the paint. Although Pike had closed the gap to 32-25 at halftime, the Red Devils were losing momentum. They had abandoned their strength, the three-point shot, in favor of penetration, and Oden was forcing their guards to miss inside.

The first time Oden touched the ball in the second half, he was mugged by three Pike defenders and called for traveling. Pike had his attention, and Oden prepared his response. He slammed home a Conley miss, then fought through a double-team for another dunk. He threw down yet another dunk on a fastbreak ignited by a Conley steal. On the other end of the court, he even took a charge to force a Pike turnover. By the time the dust had settled on the third quarter, Lawrence North had built a comfortable 12-point lead, 42-30.

But Pike made another run in the fourth quarter. Cheatham hit a three, and Pike converted a steal into a transition lay-up to climb back within eight points. The Red Devils continued to claw away at Lawrence North's lead when Teague and Cheatham sank a pair of threes to pull Pike even closer at 47-42. Lawrence North was bending but refused to break. Oden scored on an offensive rebound, and shortly thereafter hit Conley underneath the basket for a lay-up that extended the Wildcat lead to nine points with three minutes left to play. Pike narrowed the margin to five points with 60 seconds remaining but could get no closer. Shortly thereafter, the buzzer sounded on Lawrence North's 63-57 win.

By an almost sheer force of will, Oden had carried his team throughout the game. Playing every second of the game, he finished with 29 points, shooting 12-for-12 from the field and 5-for-5 from the free-throw line. He added nine rebounds, five blocks, and four assists. That was on top of shooting 6-for-6 that afternoon against Carmel, making his field goal percentage a perfect 100 percent on the day.

Coach Bullington knew he was taking a risk in not doubling or tripling down on Oden with consistency, and he got burned. After the game, he told *The Indianapolis Star* that Oden was simply too much for his team to handle. "We knew tonight's game, especially from Lawrence North's perspective, was the state championship," he said. "There's nobody else that can touch them. Playing with five guards, we had them sweating, but the big fella, he's going to be on TV on Sundays and have a great career in the NBA."

Coach Keefer was happy to have survived. "I think this is the hardest day of basketball in the nation," he said after the game. "We're expected to play two teams that are well coached, two teams that are very good, in the same day with what, three to four hours' rest? To get through today was a major obstacle course."

Lawrence North now had its biggest obstacle out of the way.

The most closely guarded secret in the state of Indiana in the week leading up to Lawrence North's semi-state matchup with Bloomington South was that Conley might not be able to play in the game. Against Pike, he took an elbow to the middle finger on his left, shooting hand on a drive to the basket. If his finger was broken, he was out. It wasn't a scenario that the Wildcats wanted to consider heading into a game against one of the few teams that had beaten them over the past four years. Two days after the Pike game, his finger was so swollen that he couldn't shoot the ball, and dribbling with his left hand was a challenge. Still, he showed up in the gym at 6:15 a.m. as usual to shoot baskets—with his *right* hand. Conley was intent on playing.

The injury turned out to be a deep bruise, and Conley was cleared to play even though he had limited use of his hand. On Friday, the day before the game, he finally gained enough flexibility in his finger to allow him to shoot left-handed, albeit uncomfortably. Still, Conley at 50 percent was better than most teams' floor generals at full health. Lawrence North would have to take solace in that fact.

After the glamour of playing in a shrine like Hinkle, it almost seemed like a letdown to play the semi-state game in the quaint gym at Southport High School just outside Indianapolis. The Wildcat team showed up in black warm-ups, and Conley kept his hand on ice, hidden under his jacket. No one noticed when he came out for warm-ups dribbling with his right hand. After a round of lay-ups, which he shot right-handed, he tried a couple of jumpers left-handed, then went to shooting right-handed from outside. He wasn't certain how he'd fare in the game with his swollen digit, so he prepared for either option.

Early in the game, Conley lofted a left-handed three-point shot. It was a "heat check," a shot intended to find out if he had a hot hand. The shot bricked off the backboard, failing to draw iron. Conley had his answer, and didn't attempt another three-point shot the entire game. But even with a bum hand, Conley still had his quickness, which he used to drive to the basket to get off right-handed lay-ups.

Lawrence North held a slim 18-15 lead in the second quarter when Oden picked up his second foul. Bloomington South decided to go right at him on their following possession to try to get him into worse foul trouble. In doing so, they abandoned their perimeter attack, which had kept them in the game to that point. Two fouls or none, Oden owned the paint, a point that he soon drove home to the Panthers by forcing them to take poor shot after poor shot.

Bloomington South was down eight points when Coach Keefer pulled Oden from the game partway through the second quarter to prevent him from picking up his third foul before the half. With Oden off the court, Conley and Windham took over the game. Windham had come of age during the tournament, possessing a double-figure scoring average and pounding the boards like a high school version of Charles Barkley. Lawrence North stretched the lead to 10 points heading into the break.

The Panthers came out focused and aggressive in the second half. They scored the first basket of the half and then followed with a three from 5-foot-8 guard Cole Holmstrom. Just like that, the Wildcat lead had been halved. But the Wildcats weren't in a giving mood: two possessions later they ran a set play that buried a dagger in Bloomington South. It was a play they hadn't tried in a while, nicknamed the "Carolina" as it was ripped from the University of North Carolina playbook. Conley brought the ball around to the left wing, and Oden moved to that side of the court as well, shifting the defensive focus along with him. McDonald snuck in behind them, darting past his defender on the weak side just as Conley lofted an alley-oop pass that McDonald caught in mid-flight for a resounding dunk. It was a statement to Bloomington South: Tonight isn't your night.

Lawrence North took the game 54-36, holding the Panthers to woeful 26-percent shooting. Oden played just 19 minutes and scored only eight points. A reporter from Columbus asked him how he thought Ohio State fans might react when they learned he had scored just eight points. "I hope they say he's a three-time state champion," Oden responded.

The night belonged to Conley, who slashed his way into the paint for 18 points shooting with his off hand. The only frustration for Conley came at the free throw line. He had 11 attempts in the game, trying the first half of them right-handed and missing every time. Finally, he reverted back to shooting left-handed from the line and made four of his free throws.

One week remained before the state finals. One week for one finger to heal. One week to wonder about *one* championship.

Nobody expected Muncie Central to return to the state finals in 2006. The Bearcats had lost all three of their three primary scoring threats from the previous season—Alex Daniel, Josiah Miller, and Ty Riddle—to graduation, and yet coach Matt Fine had led them to a 20-5 record and a rematch with Lawrence North for the 4-A championship.

Muncie Central had given the Wildcats a tough game in the 2005 finals, losing by just nine points. This year, they once again featured a balanced offensive attack, but they didn't have a single starter taller than 6-foot-5. Lawrence North expected the Bearcats to try to slow down the pace, a favorite game plan against the Wildcats. The problem with that strategy was that Lawrence North had successfully adjusted to it. When opponents lowered the number of possessions in a game, it now actually worked in Lawrence North's favor, because Oden was shooting 76 percent from the field and the team overall was hitting 60 percent of their shots. The Wildcats defense had been deadly in the tournament, and for the season their opponents were shooting just 36 percent from the field. With the Wildcats shooting so efficiently and their opponents struggling to score, it wasn't difficult to see why opponents were foolish to purposefully limit their scoring chances.

The Wildcat coaching staff kept its practices leading up to the title game brief in an effort to keep their players fresh. Conley's finger on his shooting hand had yet to fully heal. And Oden had re-injured the wrist on his shooting arm during the Bloomington

South game. After taking it easy on everyone in practice, the coaches almost had a collective heart attack when they learned that Owen was going down to the YMCA after practice and spending three hours a night playing in what they called the "beer and pizza league." They warned him, "You're about to play the biggest game of your life, so save it for the game."

Lawrence North felt prepared to face Muncie Central a second time, but worried about what steps the Bearcats had taken to ready for them. Following the 2005 title game, Coach Keefer discovered that the Muncie Central coaching staff had met with Arlington coach Larry Nicks and North Central coach Doug Mitchell prior to the championship game to discuss strategy. Wildcat coaches didn't know if a similar meeting was being held this year, but they did know that it hadn't helped Muncie's cause last year.

In their Conseco Fieldhouse locker room prior to the tip-off, none of the Wildcat staff or its players spoke about history. No one discussed the excitement of potentially winning their 45th game in a row to tie the Crispus Attucks record. No one mentioned the undefeated season that was on the line. No one talked about winning a third straight championship. Yet everyone understood the pressure they were under. That much was certain; under the surface, the significance of this night was not lost on the Wildcats.

Coach Keefer paced the room to work off his nervous energy. He told one of his assistants, "You know, if we would have gotten beat four games ago, I wouldn't be mad. But I'll tell you what, if we lose this game, I'm going to be *pissed*." In his pregame talk, Keefer went through his normal routine, discussing the game plan one final time. Lawrence North would key on Muncie Central's top scorer, Terry Jenkins, a 6-foot-3 guard who had averaged 17.6 points a game that season, and junior guard Ben Botts. But mostly, Keefer talked about his team, not the opponent. Throughout the playoffs he had stressed to his players that they had only to let their instincts take over. He pleaded with them to have an open-gym mentality, to go out and have fun and play hard. The last thing he wanted was to have them feel the weight of history bearing down on them at that moment.

But Conley had other thoughts. When Keefer asked his leader to speak, Conley rose and said, "History is going to be made here in this game. Either we're going to make history with three straight championships, or they're going to make history by beating us. And I'm not going to be no part of *Hoosiers*, Part Two."

As the Wildcats took to the court for their warm-ups, they were met with an electric atmosphere inside Conseco. Yet they appeared relaxed, smiling and joking with each other during warm-ups. Tonight was just another open gym. Their attitude was not lost on Coach Scott, who commented, "I don't think I've ever seen them so loose."

Coach Shelt and Conley shared their usual pregame ritual. Conley always wore a set of rubber bands on his wrist during warm-ups. Prior to the introductions of the starting line-ups, he'd walk over and hand them to Shelt to keep until after the game. They nodded at each other and touched fists. "Go get 'em, Mike," Shelt said. And that's precisely what he did.

Oden won the jump ball, tipping it to Conley, who pitched it to Windham for a lay-in. Instant offense. Then Conley stole the ball and drove to the hoop for an uncontested lay-up. Lawrence North was up 4-0 and had yet to run an offensive play. By the end of the quarter, Conley had nailed a three-point shot and scored on three other driving lay-ups to put Lawrence North up 24-7. In a game for the state championship, they had already tripled their opponent's score in the first quarter. While Conley sparked the team from the perimeter with 16 first-half points, Oden was scoring with ease down low on his way to a game-high 26 points. At halftime, Lawrence North had already scored 50 points to the Bearcats' 24.

Even though the game had been all but decided in the first quarter, Coach Keefer kept the starters in the line-up until the game's final 90 seconds. Possibly he wasn't ready to let go. This was, after all, the last time he would coach Oden and Conley at Lawrence North. As his stars headed for the bench, the massive Lawrence North crowd offered them a standing ovation. Oden and Conley were swarmed by their teammates as they reached the bench. Moments later, the final buzzer sounded on the Wildcats' 80-56 victory. For just the third time in Indiana high school history, a basketball team had won its third straight championship.

After receiving their medals and the championship trophy, the players boarded the bus to return to the Lawrence North gym for a late-night pep rally. But along the way, they had to make an important pit stop. A friend of Coach Keefer's was waiting to give the players a lift the rest of the way home. Keefer herded everyone out of the bus and onto their new set of wheels, a classic red fire truck. "I'm from a small town, Oak Hill," he told his team. "And in Oak Hill, whenever you win something, you get on the back of a fire truck and you ride through town." And so they did.

At the pep rally, Coach Shelt walked up to Conley to hand him his rubber bands. Conley looked at him and smiled. "I guess this will be the last time we do this, Coach." Shelt hugged him tight.

It was a moment filled with sadness that such a beautiful thing had to come to an end. But more importantly, it was a moment of intense pride.

The coach who had grown up without a father figure, and later grown into a father figure for his players, was fighting through similar emotions. "It's time," Keefer said after the game. "It's time for them to move on."

But not before they got their *one*.

Greg Oden holds the 2006 Gatorade Player of the Year trophy. AP/WWP

EPILOGUE

The beauty of the movie *Hoosiers* is that it was able to perfectly capture the spirit and character of the people of Indiana, who really do live and breathe basketball. You actually can drive through the countryside and see kids shooting hoops at a basket nailed to the side of a barn. There are 7,000-seat gymnasiums in towns that have populations of 4,000, and the stands will be filled at every game. Basketball is ingrained in the culture.

To such fans, the 2005-06 Lawrence North Wildcats will no doubt go down as one of the legendary teams in the history of Indiana high school basketball, and debates will rage for years as to whether they were the greatest ever. It will be difficult to argue against them. The Wildcats ended up ranked No. 1 in the country in both the *Sports Illustrated* and *USA Today* polls. They finished with an unblemished 29-0 record, winners of three straight titles.

Over Oden and Conley's career, the Wildcats had won 103 games and lost just seven.

Over their three years playing in the title game, Lawrence North set a host of state finals records for 4-A play: largest margin of victory (24 points); most points scored (80); most points in a half (50); most points in a quarter (26); fewest points allowed (29); highest team field goal percentage (.615); most field goals made (33); and most assists (16). Most importantly to Coach Keefer and Lawrence North—all of those records were *team* records.

One of the remarkable things about both Greg Oden and Mike Conley was the steady improvement they showed over their four years at Lawrence North. After arriving as an atrocious free throw shooter, Oden shot 79.3 percent from the line his senior year. The once timid freshman averaged 22 points and 10.5 rebounds a game as a senior, won the state's coveted Trester Award for mental attitude and academic excellence, was named Indiana's Mr. Basketball, and was chosen National Player of the Year for the second straight season. Conley raised his scoring average to 16.3 points per game as a senior, while maintaining his 4.1 assists-per-game average. For his efforts, he was named to McDonald's All-America team, along with Oden.

But life would have to go on without the devastating duo. A couple of weeks after the championship game, Coach Keefer and his staff started to prepare for the 2006-07 season. Lawrence North would begin the first year of the post Oden-Conley era against the traditional season-opening opponent, Lawrence Central, with the chance to set a new record for consecutive wins. Win No. 46 would eclipse the 50-year-old record.

The 2006-07 Wildcats will look drastically different from their predecessor. For starters, there will be a 7-foot hole in the center of the lane where Oden once stood. All told, the team is losing a total of six seniors. But despite such significant losses, they will remain formidable. Damian Windham is returning after averaging 8.4 points and 5.5 rebounds a game as a junior, his first year as a starter. He will be expected to carry the scoring burden. Also returning is Qadr Owen, who will be counted upon to fill Conley's shoes as team leader. Wesley Smith, a sweet-shooting 6-foot-3 forward, will need to have a big impact as a senior. A pair of incoming sophomores, Stephan Van Treese and Chris Read, will need to give the team valuable minutes down low. And incoming 6-foot-8 freshman Dominic Ferguson is expected to battle for a spot in the rotation.

The 2006-07 season will undoubtedly have a much different feel for the Wildcats. Out of the national spotlight, they will likely be just another high school team hoping to win their sectional. And that's okay with Lawrence North. "I just want to be a coach," Jim Etherington told the other assistants after the season. "ESPN, all this stuff, I don't need it. I just want to come in the gym and coach my kids."

As for Jack Keefer, who was named National Coach of the Year by *USA Today*, the 2006-07 season will mark his 31st year as head coach at Lawrence North. He has now coached four state champion teams; only former Marion coach Bill Green has won more, at five. At the age of 62, Keefer faces his biggest challenge yet: picking up the pieces after one unbelievable four-year run. With so many uncertainties in the personnel department, Keefer will have his hands full. His rival coaches, who have taken a beating from Lawrence North as of late, will all be licking their chops to face off against the Wildcats next season.

Keefer will welcome the challenge. After all, he'll still have a legacy to defend, just as his former stars, Oden and Conley, will have their own legacies to chase.

ACKNOWLEDGMENTS

This book would not have been possible without the cooperation of many persons, particularly Lawrence North basketball coach Jack Keefer, who never refused a request over the past three years. Assistant coaches who made major contributions included Ralph Scott, Jim Etherington, and Joe Leonard.

Mike and René Conley also were invaluable, as were Mike Conley Jr. and Greg Oden. They often gave freely of their time for extensive interviews. Others who went above and beyond the call of duty were Bill Hensley, Garry Donna, Ed Siegel, and Sonny Vaccaro.

Jimmy and Travis Smith were a tremendous help in chronicling Greg Oden's years in Terre Haute. We greatly appreciate Jim Brunner's efforts in getting us background information about Marion's triple state champions, and thank Dennis Kasey for tapes he gave us of several Lawrence North games. Very useful information about Franklin's triple state champs was provided by the book *The Franklin Wonder Five* by Phillip Ellett.

Extra-special thanks go to my co-authors, J.R. Shelt and Scott Freeman, and to Dean Smith, an NCAA coaching legend.

—Dave Krider

People come into our lives for a reason—they are a godsend. My strong passion for photography, especially sports, began by witnessing the drive of young people playing their hardest for a team victory. That passion is supported by my family and friends, and I must thank some special people who are very instrumental in my success: my family, especially my wife, LaRonda Dixon; my daughter, Aueyia Dixon; my sister, Pam Graves; and my friends Aaron Jones, Joe Britton, Sam Riche, Matt Kryger, and Mike Patton. Special thanks to the Lawrence North coaching staff and athletic directors for granting me total access to a very special team.

To my mentor, Mpozi Mshale Tolbert: Thanks for sharing your knowledge of life and in the field of photography, which we both love. Posie, thank you for your inspiration and for making a difference in my life. Rest in peace.

—David Dixon, Next Level 1
Dixon lent several of his photographs to Uncaged.

Celebrate the Heroes of Indiana Sports
in These Other Releases from Sports Publishing!

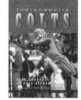

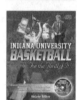